English Skills 6
Answers

Carol Matchett

Schofield&Sims

Which book?

The **English Skills** books are aligned with the end-of-year objectives for Key Stage 2. For the majority of pupils aged seven to 11 years, follow the guidance given on page 2 as to which book to use with each year group.

If a pupil is working significantly above or below the standard normally expected for his or her age, another book may be more appropriate. If you are not sure which to choose, **Workbook descriptors** and a simple **Entry test** are available to help you identify the book that is best suited to the pupil's abilities. You can also use these resources with new pupils joining your class or school.

Photocopy masters of the **Workbook descriptors** and **Entry test** are provided in the **Teacher's Guide** – which also contains the **Entry test marking key**, full instructions for use, and a range of other **English Skills** copymasters. For ordering details, see page 46.

You may be using **English Skills** at Key Stage 3 or with other mixed-ability groups of young people or adults. In such cases you will find the **Workbook descriptors** and **Entry test** vital in deciding which book to give each student.

Published by Schofield & Sims Ltd,
Dogley Mill, Fenay Bridge, Huddersfield HD8 0NQ, UK
Telephone 01484 607080

www.schofieldandsims.co.uk

Author: Carol Matchett
Carol Matchett has asserted her moral right under the Copyright, Designs and Patents Act, 1988, to be identified as the author of this work.

British Library Cataloguing in Publication Data
A catalogue record for this book is available from the British Library.

Commissioning and editorial project management by
Carolyn Richardson Publishing Services (www.publiserve.co.uk)

Design by **Ledgard Jepson Ltd**
Printed in the UK by **Wyndeham Gait Ltd**, Grimsby, Lincolnshire

Book 6 Answers ISBN 978 07217 1186 7

Contents

Schofield & Sims English Skills 6 Answers

SECTION 1

Spelling: Spelling familiar words. Distinguishing homophones. Vowel choices. Tricky letter strings/phonemes/graphemes. Silent letters. Soft **c** and **g**. Spelling polysyllabic words. Unstressed vowels. Choosing/adding prefixes and suffixes. Pluralisation. **i** before **e**.

Word structure: Identifying roots and affixes; antonym prefixes; meaning of prefixes. Word families. Using suffixes to change word class; choosing the correct suffix.

Vocabulary: Word meanings in different contexts. Archaic language. Word origins. Commonly-confused words.

Sentence structure: Varying sentence length and type; forming complex sentences. Embedding information. Varying sentence construction. Conditional sentences. Using passives.

Punctuation: Using punctuation to mark boundaries between/within sentences. Using apostrophes. Using colons, dashes and semi-colons.

Grammar: Pre- and post-noun modification. Writing inferentially. Using verbs, nouns, adjectives to create effects.

SECTION 2

Spelling: Reinforcing spelling rules, complex patterns and exceptions. Choosing endings. Single/double consonants. Common confusions.

Word structure: Hyphenation. Complex affix formations. Working out meaning using word structure/analogy to known words. Effects of suffixes.

Vocabulary: Using a dictionary/thesaurus. Inferring meaning of unknown words.

Sentence structure: Subordinate clauses using conjunctions, relative pronouns, non-finite verbs. Using modals. Passives to alter focus.

Punctuation: Using sophisticated punctuation in complex sentences/to link ideas. Integrating correctly punctuated speech in longer sentences.

Grammar: Grammatical features of text types. Pronouns. Ambiguity. Adverbs. Standard English. Similes and personification.

SECTION 3

Spelling: Complex irregular words. Identifying tricky parts. Less-common plural endings. Using analogies to known words/roots. Subject-specific homophones. Commonly-confused words. Identifying misspellings.

Word structure: Lexical patterns relating to suffixes. Using word roots/families to find meanings. Spelling errors related to prefixes/suffixes.

Vocabulary: Using words with precision in different contexts; word class/usage (e.g., words that can be both verbs and nouns; terms of qualification).

Sentence structure: Sentences for specific effects. Avoiding ambiguity.

Punctuation: Punctuation to clarify meaning or create effects.

Grammar: Grammatical confusions (e.g., less/fewer). Visual/sound effects of language. Emotive language. Connectives/text signposts.

Teacher's notes

Introduction to the series

Schofield & Sims English Skills provides regular and carefully-graded practice in key literacy skills. It is designed for use alongside your existing literacy lessons, embedding key aspects of grammar, sentence structure, punctuation and spelling and constantly revisiting them until they become automatic. At the same time it reinforces and develops pupils' knowledge of word structure and vocabulary.

Each workbook comprises three sections with 12 tests in each one. The tests become more difficult, but the increase in difficulty is gradual. The workbooks are fully compatible with the Key Stage 2 literacy curriculum and the final tests in each book are aligned with the end-of-year objectives as follows:

- **Book 1:** Year 2
- **Book 2:** Year 3
- **Book 3:** Year 4
- **Book 4:** Year 5
- **Book 5:** Year 6
- **Book 6:** Years 6/7

Please note: Pupils working towards the objectives for an earlier year should use the appropriate workbook. There is no need for all members of the class to be working on the same book at the same time.

Parts A, B and C

Each test is divided into three parts:

- Part A: **Warm-up** – puzzles, 'warm-up' exercises and revision of earlier learning
- Part B: **Word work** – spelling, word structure, exploring words and their meanings
- Part C: **Sentence work** – putting words together to make sentences: for example, choosing suitable words, forming and punctuating sentences or checking for grammatical accuracy.

Answering the test questions

After you have demonstrated to the class how some of the different question types are to be answered, the pupils work through the test items without adult help – either individually or in pairs. For Books 2 to 6, encourage them to refer to dictionaries, thesauruses and other reference materials rather than asking for your help. The tests may be used flexibly. For example, a test may be tackled in one session or over several days.

Marking

This book provides correct answers for **English Skills 6**; where various different answers would be acceptable, an example is provided. The **Focus** panel stating the areas of learning being tested helps you to decide whether the pupil's answer is satisfactory. **Please note and explain to the class that if all or part of a question has several possible answers, the question number is displayed like this 5 . If a question has a specific answer, the question number is displayed like this 5 . It is displayed in this way even if the answer is made up of several parts that may be given in any order.**

Some questions test more than one area: for example, a question on writing in the past tense might also check pupils' knowledge of the spelling rules for adding **ed**. In such cases, both parts of the answer must be correct, reflecting real-life situations that require varied knowledge and skills.

Group marking sessions

Group or class marking sessions led by the teacher or classroom assistant are the most effective way of marking the tests: pupils learn by comparing and discussing answers.

Another benefit of group or class marking sessions is that they highlight deficits in pupils' knowledge, which will inform your future teaching. Where pupils have given a wrong answer, or none at all, briefly reinforce the key teaching point using an item from this book as a model. In a plenary discussion at the end of the session, encourage pupils to evaluate their own successes; each pupil can then work with a 'talk partner' to record areas needing improvement and discuss appropriate learning objectives.

Marking the end-of-section assessments

At the end of each workbook section are two writing assessments: the independent writing task and the proofreading task. These check that pupils are applying in their writing the knowledge, skills and understanding developed in the weekly tests. The assessments also provide evidence of a pupil's strengths and weaknesses, which will help you to set appropriate targets. You might consider sharing with the pupils a simplified version of the mark scheme – and then involve them in setting their own targets, as discussed above.

• *The independent writing task*

The independent writing task gives you a snapshot of a pupil's writing development. Prompts help pupils to plan and gather ideas so that when they begin writing they can focus on expressing their ideas clearly and effectively. On pages 16, 30 and 44 you will find photocopiable **Writing task assessment sheets** – one for each section – with specific assessment points arranged under the headings 'Sentence structure and punctuation', 'Composition and effect' and 'Spelling'. Complete one of these sheets as you mark each pupil's work.

• *The proofreading task*

The proofreading task focuses on punctuation, grammar and spelling. Examples of **Completed proofreading tasks** for each section, also photocopiable, are supplied on pages 17, 31 and 45. However, please note that pupils may choose to correct some of the errors using methods different to those shown in the example but equally valid. For example, two unpunctuated strings of words might be joined using a connective or separated to make two sentences. Additional evidence gained from the relevant proofreading task will help you to further assess pupils' achievements in 'Sentence punctuation' and 'Spelling' as already assessed in the writing task. If you wish, you can use the photocopiable sheet to make notes on a pupil's work.

Please note: Pupils whose scores against the assessment statements are low do not need to repeat a section. All the books revisit difficult areas and offer ample opportunities for further practice. Instead of holding a pupil back, highlight the assessment statements that reveal his or her weaknesses and use these to set learning targets. Ensure that pupils know their targets as they begin the next section.

Progress chart

On page 46 of the pupil workbook only you will find a **Progress chart**, with one column each for Sections 1, 2 and 3, and a list of 'I can' statements relating to the kinds of activities practised in the section. Please ask every pupil to complete the relevant column when they have finished working through a section.

The **Progress chart** encourages pupils to monitor their own work by identifying those activities that they have mastered and those requiring further attention. When pupils colour in the chart as recommended (**green** for **easy**, **orange** for **getting there** and **red** for **difficult**) it gives a clear picture of progress. It also shows the benefits of systematic practice: an activity that the pupil cannot perform in Section 1 later gets the 'green light'.

The **Progress chart** promotes assessment for learning and personalised learning. Whilst it is best completed in the workbook, so that achievements in all sections may be compared, you may at some point wish to have additional copies. For this reason, it may be photocopied. **However, all other pages of the pupil workbook remain strictly non-photocopiable.**

Section 1   Test 1

A   WARM-UP

hall paint

Use these words to write

1 **a complex sentence:** Lucy noticed the smell of wet paint as soon as she entered the hall.

2 **a question:** Is the paint in the hall still wet?

Write two adverbs that give contrasting pictures.

3 She got up _energetically_ / _painfully_ .

4 He smiled _sheepishly_ / _menacingly_ .

5 He spoke _politely_ / _angrily_ .

6 She stood _dejectedly_ / _proudly_ .

Underline the hidden four-, five- or six-letter word.

7 S P T E <u>S U R E</u> P L D E

8 D A <u>W F U L</u> T H O S K

9 C L S C H O L <u>W E I R D</u> L E

10 C H E <u>C T I C L E</u> N P L E

PART A Focus
1–2: sentence types
3–6: using adverbs for effect
7–10: visual spelling strategies

B   WORD WORK

Complete the verb table.

		+ ing	+ ed
1	control	controlling	controlled
2	happen	happening	happened

Complete the adjective table.

		+ y	+ er	+ est
3	fun	funny	funnier	funniest
4	ice	icy	icier	iciest

Write the word showing its root word and affixes.

5 immortality   im / mortal / ity

6 inexpensive   in / expense / ive

PART B Focus
1–4: spelling rules; word endings
5–6: word structure
7–10: homophones

Underline the correct word.

7 The driver was (<u>braking</u> / breaking) hard.

8 Two eagles (saw / sore / <u>soar</u>) overhead.

9 There was a (freeze / <u>frieze</u>) on the wall.

10 The words in brackets are called homophones because they sound the same but have different spellings and meanings.

C   SENTENCE WORK

Add subordinate clauses to the beginning, middle and end of the sentence.

1 _Squirming with embarrassment,_ Zack looked away quickly.

2 Zack, _sickened by what he saw,_ looked away quickly.

3 Zack looked away quickly _before anyone noticed._

PART C Focus
1–3: varying the position of subordinate clauses
4–5: commas, full stops and capital letters for clarity and effect
6–10: using prepositional phrases to enhance meaning

Add the commas, full stops and capital letters.

4 ^W^waiting for Sita, Jenny saw a man leaving the house. ^S^~~s~~he had seen him before. ^H^~~he~~ had been in the car that night.

5 ^W^~~we~~ make needless car journeys, leave countless electrical appliances on standby and waste the world's natural resources ^Y^yet no-one seems to care.

Add a prepositional phrase after the noun so that the directions are clear.

6 Look for a gate _between the two cottages on the left._

7 Cross the stream _on a wooden bridge._

8 Head for the stile _in the corner of the field._

9 Turn left through a gate _at the top of the hill._

10 Follow the path _along the side of the farm buildings._

4   X DEFINITIVE ANSWER   X SAMPLE ANSWER

Section 1 Test 2

A WARM-UP

Make the sentence into a compound sentence.

1 Joe was lost _and no-one knew where he was._

2 There was a crash _but after that I remember nothing._

3 She spun round _and there was Glen._

Underline the word that is spelt correctly.

4 color sorce <u>score</u> contor

5 wership werse <u>fern</u> jernal

Write correctly the words that are wrongly spelt.

6 4: _colour, source, contour_

7 5: _worship, worse, journal_

Complete the words to make a word that ends and a word that starts with the root.

8 _auto_ graph   graph _ic_

9 _tri_ dent   dent _ist_

10 _trans_ port   port _folio_

B WORD WORK

1 Underline the words that have a soft **c**.

<u>decision</u> critic <u>process</u> cursor

<u>incisor</u> score <u>cancel</u> <u>mercy</u>

2 A soft **c** is usually followed by the letters _'y', 'i' or 'e'._

3 Add **c** or **s**.

coun _c_ il   jui _c_ y   in _s_ ect   pro _c_ ess

ten _s_ e   sy _s_ tem   re _c_ ipe   re _s_ ult

4 Add the correct antonym prefix.

_un_ familiar   _in_ attentive

_im_ probable   _non_ -violent

Use a prefix to write the word that means

5 not noticed: _unnoticed_

6 not regular: _irregular_

7 not legal: _illegal_

8 not mature: _immature_

Write a sentence that shows the meaning.

9 minor: _It was only a minor alteration._

10 miner: _My grandfather was a coal miner who worked in the pits all his life._

C SENTENCE WORK

Write a complex sentence starting with the non-finite verb.

1 Hobbling _painfully, Scarlet made for the cover of the trees._

2 Stunned _by the discovery, George wanted some time to think._

3 Realising _his mistake, Harry had to reassess the situation._

4 Hounded _by guilt, Laura could not sleep._

Explain why a dash has been used in each example.

5 The porridge was cold and lumpy – yuck! _To add a comment._

6 Lucy clambered to her feet – she was not defeated yet. _It creates a dramatic pause._

7 "I thought I heard –" began Ricky. _Indicates an interruption in direct speech._

Write a sentence to show how the tense might be used in a promotional leaflet describing a stately home.

8 past: _The main house was built in 1756._

9 present: _The house is open to the public at weekends._

10 future: _You will enjoy the colour and aroma of the exotic gardens._

Section 1 Test 3

A WARM-UP

Continue each sentence using a different subordinating connective.

1 Ben smiled <u>despite the pain.</u>

2 Ben smiled <u>as Jack told his story.</u>

3 Ben smiled <u>in case we thought he was</u> <u>scared.</u>

Complete the well-known saying.

> **PART A Focus**
> 1–3: complex sentences, subordinating connectives
> 4–6: use of apostrophes
> 7–10: vowel choices

4 <u>Don't</u> give up the day job.

5 Crime <u>doesn't</u> pay.

6 You <u>can't</u> take it with you.

7 Add the same grapheme to all the words.

<u>au</u> tumn   appl <u>au</u> se   s <u>au</u> sage   <u>au</u> dience

8 Which word sounds different?

<u>sausage</u>

9 Add the same grapheme to all the words.

<u>ea</u> sel   m <u>ea</u> gre   l <u>ea</u> gue   w <u>ea</u> lth

10 Which word sounds different?

<u>wealth</u>

B WORD WORK

Add the missing vowels.

1 gall <u>e</u> ry   fact <u>o</u> ry   libr <u>a</u> ry   qu <u>a</u> y

2 pen <u>a</u> lty   inj <u>u</u> ry   troph <u>y</u>   voll <u>e</u> y

Write all the words as plurals.

3 1: <u>galleries, factories, libraries, quays</u>

4 2: <u>penalties, injuries, trophies, volleys</u>

5 Make six words using these word parts only.

contra pre re dict view tion

<u>contradict, predict, preview, review,</u>
<u>contradiction, prediction</u>

> **PART B Focus**
> 1–2: vowel choice
> 3–4: pluralisation (y endings)
> 5–8: using prefixes/roots
> 9–10: common confusions

Write the meaning of the prefix.

6 contra: <u>against</u>   **8** re: <u>again</u>

7 pre: <u>before</u>

Write a sentence that shows the meaning.

9 bought: <u>I've been shopping today and I</u> <u>bought some new jeans.</u>

10 brought: <u>I've brought some photos to</u> <u>show you.</u>

C SENTENCE WORK

Complete the conditional sentence using one of these words. Use a different word in each sentence.

if, as long as, provided that, unless

1 There will be a drought <u>unless it rains soon.</u>

2 People will come to the car boot sale <u>as long as it stays dry.</u>

3 There is no danger <u>provided that you follow the guidelines.</u>

4 Jackson would have won <u>if he had been fully fit.</u>

Add the missing comma or commas. Give a reason for their use.

5 You will come to the party, won't you? <u>To attach a question tag to a statement.</u>

6 Busy writing, she hardly noticed Jo enter. <u>To separate the parts of a complex sentence.</u>

7 The third woman had red hair, a thin face, steely eyes and an unpleasant snarl.
<u>To separate descriptive phrases in a list.</u>

8 In conclusion, this would seem to be the way forward. <u>To mark off the connecting phrase.</u>

9 Underline the verbs.

Jack <u>whirled</u> round, <u>slipping</u> in the mud, <u>grasping</u> a branch.

> **PART C Focus**
> 1–4: conditional sentences; tense
> 5–8: commas to clarify meaning
> 9–10: verbs to create effects

10 What effect is created by the verbs used?

<u>The list of verbs suggests that the character is making desperate movements.</u>

⬚ **X** DEFINITIVE ANSWER   **X** SAMPLE ANSWER

Section 1 Test 4

A WARM-UP

Write three sentences describing different aspects of the same **door**.

1 simple: *The door was locked.*

2 compound: *It had been painted once but now the paint was blistered and peeling.*

3 complex: *Although it had a small window, the glass was so grimy that there was no chance of seeing in or out.*

Continue the compound word chain.

4 internet – **net** *work* – *workshop*

5 high**light** – *lighthouse* – *houseboat*

6 further**more** – *moreover* – *overlook*

Write as a word.

7 40 *forty*

8 8th *eighth*

9 90 *ninety*

10 12th *twelfth*

> **PART A Focus**
> **1–3:** varying sentence length and structure
> **4–6:** word structure; compound words
> **7–10:** high-frequency words

B WORD WORK

Write the words correctly.

1 easly *easily*   desprate *desperate*

2 Cathlic *Catholic*   journlist *journalist*

3 What is wrong with all the misspelt words?
The unstressed vowel is missing.

4 What technique might help you to remember the correct spellings?
Emphasising the three syllables when you say the word.

Underline the word that is spelt correctly.

5 definatly <u>definitely</u> definately

6 entrence enterance <u>entrance</u>

7 Add the same consonant suffix to each word.
command *ment* advertise *ment* settle *ment*

8 The suffix changes the verbs into *nouns* .

9 Add the same vowel suffix to each word.
acid *ic*   photograph *ic*   athlete *ic*

10 The suffix changes the nouns into *adjectives* .

> **PART B Focus**
> **1–6:** unstressed vowels
> **7–10:** using suffixes to change word class

C SENTENCE WORK

1 Rewrite the sentence in the passive form.
The third marquis built the house. *The house was built by the third marquis.*

2 How is the passive version different? *The active sentence is about what the marquis did; the passive sentence is about the house.*

Rewrite the headline in the passive form.

3 Snake bites man   *Man bitten by snake*

4 Council closes Skate Park   *Skate Park closed by council*

Sam is scared of Marcie. Show this

5 **using a line of dialogue:** *"Of course I'll help you, Marcie," whispered Sam, her voice trembling.*

6 **by describing the behaviour of the character/s:** *Sam froze when she heard Marcie call her name.*

Add a colon and complete the sentence.

7 There are three main types of sentence: *simple, compound and complex.*

8 This is how my favourite poem begins: *Slowly, silently, now the moon*

9 There is only one option: *leave before it is too late.*

10 Final score: *4–0 to England.*

> **PART C Focus**
> **1–4:** effects of using active and passive
> **5–6:** writing inferentially; portraying character
> **7–10:** using colons

Section 1 Test 5

A WARM-UP

Write a sentence to show how the tense might be used in an autobiography.

1 past: I was born in London in 1973.

2 present: Now I live in Devon.

3 future: Next year I will move to France.

> **PART A Focus**
> 1–3: shifting tense for specific purpose
> 4–8: antonym prefixes; spelling patterns
> 9–10: visual spelling strategies

Underline the antonym.

4 regular <u>irregular</u> unregular iregular

5 literate inliterate <u>illiterate</u> unliterate

6 appear dissappear <u>disappear</u> reappear

7 named unamed illnamed <u>unnamed</u>

8 inform disinform uninform <u>misinform</u>

9 Add a short word to complete the longer word.

comfor <u>table</u>   env <u>iron</u> ment   a <u>post</u> rophe

10 Add the same short word to complete all three longer words.

lis <u>ten</u> ing   po <u>ten</u> tial   in <u>ten</u> sive

B WORD WORK

Add the suffix **ly**.

1 love <u>ly</u>   sure <u>ly</u>   actual <u>ly</u>

2 whole <u>ly</u>   responsible <u>y</u>   able <u>y</u>

3 Write the meaning of the prefix.

auto: <u>self</u>

prim(us): <u>first</u>

trans: <u>across</u>

Write three words derived from the prefix.

4 auto automobile, autograph, automatic

5 prim primary, prime, primrose

6 trans transfer, transplant, transform

Write the modern word that means the same.

7 nay: no

8 thou: you

9 thee: you

10 hast: have

> **PART B Focus**
> 1–2: modifying spelling when adding **ly**
> 3–6: using knowledge of classic prefixes
> 7–10: archaic language

C SENTENCE WORK

Rewrite the sentence so that the information given in brackets is embedded within it.

> **PART C Focus**
> 1–3: embedding information
> 4–8: use and misuse of commas; comma splice
> 9–10: understanding terms; point of view

1 Rosalind was completely fearless. (She was elderly.)

Rosalind, though elderly, was completely fearless.

2 His trainers were now ruined. (They were brand new.)

His trainers, which were brand new, were now ruined.

3 Mr Khan shuffled from behind the counter. (He was grumbling under his breath.)

Mr Khan, grumbling under his breath, shuffled from behind the counter.

Put a tick if the comma is used correctly. Put a cross if it is not.

4 It was getting dark, the bus was late.   <u>X</u>

5 The animals fled, scenting fear and death.   <u>✓</u>

6 France is an interesting country, the scenery is beautiful.   <u>X</u>

7 This book is great, you should read it.   <u>X</u>

8 Explain why some commas were used incorrectly. Two main clauses cannot be linked with a comma.
They need something stronger, such as a full stop or a semi-colon.

Write a definition.

9 biased: taking one point of view   **10 balanced:** presenting fairly both sides of an argument

8   X DEFINITIVE ANSWER   X SAMPLE ANSWER

Section 1 Test 6

A WARM-UP

Write a slogan for a new place to eat called
Dan's Diner. Use

1 **alliteration:** Dan's diner – delectable,
delicious and divine

2 **rhyme:** There's nothing finer
Than eating at Dan's diner

3 **word play:** It's Dan-tastic!

Complete the rhyming homophone pairs.

4 **bear** and b are / m ayor and m are

5 **right** and write / s ite and s ight

6 **meat** and meet / b eet and b eat

7 **wait** and weight / gr ate and gr eat

PART A Focus
1–3: language sound effects
4–8: homophones
9–10: pluralisation

8 Write the homophone.

story storey   **beach** beech

9 Write the plurals of all four words.
stories, storeys, beaches, beeches

10 Underline the word that is the same in singular
and plural form.
mouse fungus <u>sheep</u> tooth

B WORD WORK

1 Complete the grid.

	+ ed	+ ing	+ er
supply	supplied	supplying	supplier
travel	travelled	travelling	traveller
ski	skied	skiing	skier

Add the missing syllables.

2 in / gre / di / ent **Clue:** listed in a recipe

3 in / gra / ti / tude **Clue:** a lack of thanks

4 in / flu / en / tial **Clue:** able to influence

5 in / ter / rup / tion **Clue:** unplanned break

PART B Focus
1: word endings; adding vowel suffixes
2–5: using syllables to work out the spelling
6–7: using the endings er and or
8–10: word origins

Add **er** or **or**.

6 curs or   comput er   monit or   sens or

7 direct or   narrat or   writ er   act or

Explain the derivation.

8 **sumo** from the Japanese sport

9 **spotlight** is a compound word made
from 'spot' and 'light'

10 **motel** combines 'motor' and 'hotel'

C SENTENCE WORK

Complete the sentence.

1 If everyone used low-energy light bulbs, it would drastically reduce energy consumption.

2 Unless we act now to slow global warming, it may soon be too late.

3 If we continue to use water at the present rate, we shall soon face water shortages.

4 What is the purpose of sentences like these? To put forward theories as to what might happen.

Rewrite the sentence, replacing the conjunction with a semi-colon.

5 I never eat peanuts because I have a nut allergy. I never eat peanuts; I have a nut allergy.

6 The dog returned for a third time so he was clearly a determined creature.
The dog returned for a third time; he was clearly a determined creature.

7 I shall not be going on the trip as we are short of money.
I shall not be going on the trip; we are short of money.

PART C Focus
1–4: conditional sentences
5–7: use of semi-colon
8–10: writing inferentially;
verbs for effect

Complete the sentences using verbs suggesting that the characters are both nervous and

8 **uncertain:** Jafar shuffled forward, staying hidden amongst the shadows.

9 **frightened:** Mick was trembling, his palms sweating and his heart racing.

10 **excited:** Backstage, the actors were whispering and giggling.

Section 1 Test 7

A WARM-UP

leaves clown

Use the words in

PART A Focus
1–3: varying sentence structure
4–6: vowel choices
7–10: anagrams; spelling strategies

1 **a simple sentence:** The clown jumped into the pile of leaves.

2 **a compound sentence:** The clown takes a bow and leaves the circus ring.

3 **a complex sentence:** As the clown leaves the circus ring, the crowd cheers.

Add the letters needed for the missing vowel sound.

4 *Clue: music*

ch or d   h ar m o ny   m e l o dy

5 *Clue: RE*

s y mb o l   w or sh i p   s a cr e d

6 *Clue: ICT*

h ar dw ar e   spr ea dsh ee t   m e m or y

Solve the anagram.

7 **hears:** share   **9** **gates:** stage

8 **skid:** disk   **10** **tough:** ought

B WORD WORK

1 Add **ie** or **ei**.

bel ie ve   f ie rce   rec ei ve   c ei ling

2 What spelling rule did you use?

'i' before 'e' except after 'c'.

3 Add **ie** or **ei**.

n ei ghbour   for ei gn   consc ie nce

4 The spelling rule does **not** apply to these words. Why? Because the 'ie' and 'ei' don't make long 'e' sounds in these words.

Add suffixes to make three more words.

5 **pity** pitiful, pitiless, pitifully

6 **fit** fitful, fitting, fitness

7 **hope** hopeful, hopeless, hoping

Sort the words according to the subject.
Some words may be used twice.

virus digest modem display
portrait sketch pastel oxygen

PART B Focus
1–4: ie and ei spelling patterns
5–7: word structure; suffix rules
8–10: subject-specific meanings

8 **ICT:** virus, modem, display, portrait

9 **science:** virus, oxygen, digest

10 **art:** display, portrait, pastel, sketch

C SENTENCE WORK

Write a sentence to show how the sentence type might be used in a promotional leaflet describing a castle.

1 **statement:** The castle was built in 1573.

PART C Focus
1–4: varying sentence types
5–8: adjectives; character impressions
9–10: using the dash for effect

2 **exclamation:** Meet the ghost of Sir Thomas!

3 **directive:** Discover the history of the Granville family.

4 **question:** What was it like to live in medieval times?

5 Underline the adjectives.

Aunt Maud was wearing her usual beige cardigan, traditional plaid skirt and sensible flat shoes.

6 What impression do they create of Aunt Maud? That she is very conventional and regular in her dress and behaviour.

Write a sentence that makes Aunt Maud sound

7 **eccentric:** Aunt Maud's outfit was a riot of colour, finished with a splash of bangles and beads.

8 **imposing:** Aunt Maud was wearing an immaculate black suit with a high starched collar.

Add a dash and continue each sentence in a dramatic and interesting way.

9 Then he heard the driver's voice – it was Mack!

10 The tomb was full of incredible treasures – so incredible that Henry could only stand and stare.

X DEFINITIVE ANSWER   X SAMPLE ANSWER

Section 1 Test 8

Write a sentence to show how the tense might be used in a discussion about the importance of exercise.

1 **past:** *Fifty years ago, people walked more because there were fewer cars.*

2 **present:** *Today, some children have no daily exercise.*

3 **future:** *There will be huge health implications in the future.*

Complete the well-known saying using the name of an animal.

4 the *cat's* whiskers **6** the *bee's* knees

5 a *dog's* dinner **7** the *lion's* share

Use the mnemonic to write three words.

8 **G**et **r**eady **a**nd **p**lay **h**ard.
graph, graphic, photograph

9 **O**h **U** **n**aughty **t**iger!
count, amount, mountain

10 **A**lways **u**se **g**ood **h**umour.
laugh, daughter, naught

PART A Focus
1–3: shifting tense for specific purpose
4–7: idioms; possessive apostrophe
8–10: mnemonics; spelling patterns

B **WORD WORK**

Underline the unstressed vowel. Then split the word to show the root word and affix.

1 pois<u>o</u>nous   poison / ous

2 r<u>e</u>ference   refer / ence

3 off<u>e</u>ring   offer / ing

4 Split each of the words into syllables.
poi / son / ous   ref / er / ence
off / er / ing

5 How do these techniques help to spell the words?
They show the unstressed vowels.

Write two words with the prefix

6 **bi** (meaning **two**): *bicycle, biceps*

7 **de** (meaning **undo**): *decode, deform*

Add the correct word.

PART B Focus
1–5: unstressed vowels
6–7: meaning of prefixes; word structure
8–10: common confusions

lighting   lightening   lightning

8 A fork of *lightning* lit up the sky.

9 The sky was *lightening* as the cloud lifted.

10 The *lighting* for the scene was perfect.

C **SENTENCE WORK**

Reorder the words to make three different sentences. **Kelly ran down the street searching frantically.**

1 *Frantically, Kelly ran down the street, searching.*

2 *Searching frantically, Kelly ran down the street.*

3 *Down the street Kelly ran, searching frantically.*

4 Which version or versions focus most effectively on Kelly's feelings?
Those where 'frantically' is near the start of the sentence.

Put a tick if the colon is used correctly. Put a cross if it is not.

5 On the desk there was: a pencil, a notebook and a telephone directory.   *X*

6 My favourite saying is: 'Look before you leap'.   *X*

7 There is only one team for me: Leeds United.   *✓*

PART C Focus
1–4: reordering sentences for effect
5–7: using the colon (following a clause that makes sense on its own)
8–10: pre- and post-noun modification

Add words or phrases before and after the nouns to modify them.

8 They reached the *impressive wrought-iron* gates *embossed with lions' faces.*

9 They found a *forgotten, overgrown* garden *behind the cottage.*

10 There was the *huge, wide-mouthed* cave, *opening onto the beach.*

11

Section 1 Test 9

A WARM-UP

Use the words to make four sentences.

Joe outside remorse filled waited with quietly

1 Joe waited quietly outside, filled with remorse.

2 Filled with remorse, Joe waited quietly outside.

3 Outside, Joe waited quietly, filled with remorse.

4 Joe, filled with remorse, waited quietly outside.

Complete the sentence, using the short word that you add to complete the longer word.

5 You can act a char act er.

6 You can hear a re hear sal.

7 You can strum stringed in strum ents.

Write a word that ends and a word that starts with the grapheme.

8 wid en en large

9 hero ic ic on

10 geogra phy phy sical

> **PART A Focus**
> 1–4: reordering sentences
> 5–7: spelling strategies; mnemonics
> 8–10: letter strings; word structure

B WORD WORK

Add the suffix **able**.

1 respect able stop pable suit able

2 envy iable rely iable pay able

3 adore able dispose able manage able

4 What class of words have you made? adjectives

5 What do you notice about the spelling of the words ending in **e**?
   Some drop the 'e'; 'manageable' keeps the 'e'.

6 Add the same letter string to each word.
   res our ce fl our col our j our ney

7 Why is this a tricky letter string? Because the letters can represent different phonemes.

> **PART B Focus**
> 1–5: modifying words; adding the suffix **able**
> 6–7: letter strings; tricky words
> 8–10: word meanings; subject-specific use

Write different definitions.

8 **score** (in PE): points won

9 **score** (in design and technology): make cuts in the surface

10 **score** (in music): a piece of music written down

C SENTENCE WORK

Rewrite as three separate sentences.

> **PART C Focus**
> 1–4: short sentences for effect
> 5–6: narrative structure; organisation
> 7–10: comma; semi-colon

Now that the wind had dropped, the house was silent and nothing stirred.

1 The wind had dropped. The house was silent now. Nothing stirred.

2 The effect of the short sentences is a building of tension.

They pounded on the door and they cried out but still there was no reply.

3 They pounded on the door. They cried out. Still there was no reply.

4 The effect of the short sentences is to create a sense of panic.

5 Give two reasons for starting a new paragraph when you are writing a story.
   Change of time or place; change of focus.

6 Here are some ways of ending a story. Write a brief note to explain each term.
   a cliffhanger: Reader left guessing. **a final twist:** An unexpected ending.
   a resolution: Main issues resolved.

Add a comma or a semi-colon.

7 Her eyes were red; she'd been crying.

8 Something lurked, waiting for me.

9 It was raining; his bare feet were cold.

10 Shivering violently, he reached out.

X DEFINITIVE ANSWER   X SAMPLE ANSWER

Section 1   Test 10

A   WARM-UP

It could snow tomorrow.

Rewrite the sentence as

1   **a headline:** Weather warning: snow threatened

2   **a rhyming couplet:**

The sky is grey, the temperature low
I really think there might be snow.

3   **a complex sentence:** If temperatures remain below 0°C, it could snow tomorrow.

Complete each word by adding

PART A Focus
1–3: sentence variation
4–6: visual spelling strategies
7–10: homophones; spelling

4   **an onomatopoeia:**

un pop ular   t hum b   neigh bour

5   **a pronoun:**

jealo us   you th   he ight

6   **a possessive pronoun:**

hum our   sp her e   my th

Write the homophone.

7   **profit** prophet   9   **rain** reign

8   **bite** byte   10   **not** knot

B   WORD WORK

Add the correct 'shun' ending.

1   conjunc tion   dimen sion   nutri tion

2   Rus sian   A sian   dieti cian

3   conserva tion   opposi tion   prepara tion

Add the same phoneme to all three words.

4   ph ysical   gra ph ic   apostro ph e

5   stoma ch   ch emist   a ch e

6   s y stem   d y nasty   rh y thm

PART B Focus
1–3: choosing the correct 'shun' suffix
4–6: tricky phonemes
7–10: meaning of words in different contexts

Write a definition of the word in **bold**.

7   a **brief** visit

brief: lasting only a short time

8   a design **brief**

brief: instructions; information about a task

9   a **current** news story

current: relating to today; correct now

10   an electric **current**

current: flow; movement

C   SENTENCE WORK

Complete the conditional sentence.

PART C Focus
1–4: use of conditional sentences
5–7: brackets; parenthesis
8–10: noun phrases chosen for effect

1   If the weather had been better, we could have gone to the beach.

2   If the river had continued to rise, the town would have flooded.

3   If Mr Higgins had not seen us, we might have got away with it.

4   What is the purpose of sentences like these?

They show what might have happened if circumstances had been different.

Add brackets.

5   In the south, summers (December to March) are cool and winters (June to September) are mild.

6   Some snakes inject venom (poison) into their prey through specially grooved fangs (teeth).

7   Using brackets like this is called _____parenthesis_____ . The brackets are used to mark off words that are not part of the main sentence.

Write a sentence using nouns and noun phrases to create an effect that is

8   **frightening:** The cellar was low and dank with shadows lurking in the corners.

9   **welcoming:** A cheerful fire was crackling in the grate giving everyone a warm glow.

10   **unusual:** The wall was a mass of computer screens, each of them flashing with streams of numbers.

Section 1 Test 11

A WARM-UP

Improve on the cliché.

1 as smooth as ~~silk~~ *the silken threads on the Emperor's finest robes*

2 as cold as ~~ice~~ *icicles gripping onto winter branches*

3 as warm as ~~toast~~ *a lizard basking in the midday heat*

Write the homophone pair.

4 a female sheep: *ewe*
   a type of tree: *yew*

5 hairless: *bald*
   wailed: *bawled*

6 a male child: *boy*
   a float or marker: *buoy*

Write a word that ends and a word that starts with each letter string.

7   *si* gn   gn *at*
8   *lea* gue   gue *st*
9   *hy* mn   mn *emonic*
10 *fan* cy   cy *linder*

PART A Focus
1–3: use of imagery
4–6: homophones
7–10: letter patterns

B WORD WORK

1 Add the missing letter.
   autum *n*   clim *b*   colum *n*

2 Write the words correctly.
   strenth *strength*   casle *castle*
   rombus *rhombus*   musle *muscle*

3 The same letter is silent in all the words. Underline it.
   s<u>c</u>enery s<u>c</u>issors cre<u>sc</u>ent resu<u>sc</u>itate

4 Explain why it is silent. *Because it is overpowered by the 's' that precedes it.*

Write two words with the same root.

5 circulate *circular, circumference*
6 audible *audition, auditorium*

Write the meaning of the root.

7 circu(m): *around*   8 audi: *hear*

Write a definition of the word in **bold**.

9 Their first attempt was **sabotaged**.
   sabotaged: *spoilt on purpose*

10 The girl had a **beguiling** manner.
    beguiling: *charming and captivating*

PART B Focus
1–4: silent consonants
5–8: common roots
9–10: definitions

C SENTENCE WORK

Rewrite the sentence in the passive form, hiding those who perform the actions.

1 The council will reverse the decision. *The decision will be reversed.*

2 Shop assistants turned many customers away. *Many customers were turned away.*

3 The keepers feed the animals twice a day. *The animals are fed twice a day.*

Add a question tag to turn the statement into a question.

4 This one is yours, *isn't it?*

5 We all want this, *don't we?*

6 You will come, *won't you?*

7 You can see my problem, *can't you?*

PART C Focus
1–3: use of the passive
4–7: question tags; use of apostrophes, commas and question marks
8–10: use of verbs for effect

8 Underline the verbs.
   Reporters <u>buzzed</u> around the office, papers <u>flying</u> from hand to hand and keyboards <u>clattering</u>.

9 What impression does this create? *A lively, busy, bustling place.*

10 Describe a place with a sleepy atmosphere.
    Old ladies dozed in chairs, lulled to sleep by the peaceful clink of teacup on saucer.

X DEFINITIVE ANSWER   X SAMPLE ANSWER

Section 1 Test 12

A WARM-UP

Write a sentence using these words.

lion net

1 active sentence: The lion tore the net with its teeth.

2 passive sentence: The net was torn to shreds by the lion.

3 question: Did the lion see the net?

4 imperative: Place the net between you and the lion.

Complete the rhyming homophone pairs.

5 air and heir ; w here and wear

6 ate and eight ; f ate and fete

7 no and Know ; s o and sew

8 threw and through ; b lue and blew

Solve the anagrams.

9 Susie: issue   **Leah:** heal

10 Bertha: breath   **Edgar:** grade

B WORD WORK

Add the same ending to both words. **ary ery ory**

1 mem ory   categ ory

2 imagin ary   sanctu ary

3 flatt ery   gall ery

4 Circle the unstressed vowel in each ending.

5 What technique would help you to remember the correct ending? Saying the words split into syllables to emphasise the vowel.

6 Underline the words that have a soft **g**.

engage mega digit energy agog

7 A soft **g** is usually followed by the letters 'e', 'i' or 'y'.

If these were real words, what would they mean? Write a definition.

8 aquaport (verb): to carry by water

9 automemory (noun): a device that remembers something automatically

10 superwealthy (adjective): very rich

C SENTENCE WORK

Combine the three sentences into one.

1 He was tired. He walked on. Then he came to the river.
Although he was tired, he walked on until he came to the river.

2 They drove past the field. Jenny waved at Billy. He was still digging.
As they drove past the field, Jenny waved at Billy – who was still digging.

3 I was walking home. I found a bag. It contained money.
Walking home, I found a bag containing money.

4 Why do the original versions sound wrong?
Every new thought has equal weight, and the effect is monotonous.

Continue the line of dialogue.

5 She sighed and then asked, "Why've you come?"

6 Peering from the window, Carrie said, "Here comes Phil."

7 A voice shouted, "Get him!"

8 Underline the abstract nouns. Su stared at him with <u>bewilderment</u> and <u>terror</u>.

9 What is the purpose of the abstract nouns? To show the mixed emotions of the character.

10 Write different abstract nouns for a different effect. Su stared at him with disgust and loathing .

Remind the pupil to complete Section 1 of the Progress chart on page 46 of the workbook. 15

Schofield & Sims English Skills 6

Section 1 Writing task assessment sheet: After hours club

Name		Class/Set	
Teacher's name		Date	

Sentence structure and punctuation

	Always/often	Sometimes	Never
Varies sentence length (e.g., short and simple for clarity or impact; complex to explain)			
Uses embedded clauses for succinctness			
Sentences constructed to express subtleties in meaning (e.g., using passives or conditionals)			
Uses appropriate and varied connectives			
Manipulates word order (e.g., adverbials or clauses) for emphasis, effect and to bring ideas to the fore			
Makes appropriate shifts between tenses and verb forms, including modals			
Maintains sentence punctuation			
Uses commas within complex sentences to mark boundaries and clarify meaning			
Uses sophisticated punctuation (semi-colon, colon, brackets, dashes)			

Composition and effect

Chooses and organises content to match the purpose of the text and the needs of the reader			
Organises ideas into a coherent sequence of paragraphs			
Each paragraph has a clear focus			
Suitable tone is maintained (formal yet enthusiastic)			
Letter is made convincing by techniques (e.g., reiteration, repetition, rhetorical questions)			
Appropriate choice of formal vocabulary			
Viewpoint is well controlled, recognising and addressing other views			

Spelling

Polysyllabic words are spelt correctly			
Correct homophones are used			
Words with unstressed vowels are spelt correctly			
Familiar letter strings are spelt correctly			
Endings are correctly chosen (e.g., **er**, **or**)			
Tricky vowels and consonants are correctly chosen (e.g., **ei/ie**, **c/s**, **y/i**)			
Rules for adding endings are correctly applied; common exceptions are recognised			
Uses apostrophes correctly			

Schofield & Sims English Skills 6

Section 1 Completed proofreading task: My favourite place

Name	Class/Set
Teacher's name	Date

I realy do'nt rememmber much about my first jerney to the casel – ownly the burning colers of the awtumn trees as we drived up the windding road and the delightfull sent of damp woodland.

I xpect Mrs Higgins was waiting to recieve us at the enterence, enquireing about our jerney and provideing us with welcomeing drinks of hot choclate. She usuly did, allthogh I can't actuly rememmber that particuler time.

What I definitly do recall quiet clearley was wakeing the next morning to the bearly audable murmmur of the wind in the trees – that's a memery I shall allways treshure.

The senary around the casel was quiet breathtakeing. for a child like me, used to sity life, living in a casel was such a huje advenchure,. I loved the forist – it was my privite advenchure playground.

I thought then, and I still think now, their is no more piecefull place or more beautifull rejion anywhere in the werld.

Section 1 tasks summary

Section 2 Test 1

A WARM-UP

Modify the noun so that it describes a particular object in detail.

1 door: _an ancient wooden door with a brass handle_

2 mirror: _the ornate mirror above the fireplace_

3 lamp: _an old-fashioned gas lamp in the hallway_

4 sandwich: _a cheese and tomato sandwich on crusty wholemeal bread_

Write another word that follows the same spelling pattern.

5 length   _strength_

6 count   _country_

7 sought   _thought_

Solve the anagram with a one-word answer.

8 Love S: _solve_

9 Love N: _novel_

10 Love W: _vowel_

> **PART A Focus**
> 1–4: noun modification
> 5–7: letter strings
> 8–10: visual spelling strategies; anagrams

B WORD WORK

Add the missing letters.

> **PART B Focus**
> 1–4: c/s and g/j confusions
> 5–6: root words and suffixes
> 7–10: commonly-confused words

1 cy sy

_cy_ clone   _sy_ stem   _sy_ mbol   _cy_ nical

2 ce se

sour _ce_   cour _se_   audien _ce_   incen _se_

3 ce se

_ce_ real   _ce_ metery   _se_ ptic   _se_ rial

4 g j

a _g_ ile   sub _j_ ect   ad _j_ acent   di _g_ est

5 Make six words using these roots and suffixes only.

pure extreme ity ify ist ism

purity, purify, purist
extremist, extremity, extremism

6 Which suffix can make a verb? _ify_

Write a definition.

7 resent (verb): _to bear a grudge about_

8 recent (adjective): _not long past_

9 stationary (adjective): _not moving_

10 stationery (noun): _materials for writing_

C SENTENCE WORK

Underline the subordinate clause.

> **PART C Focus**
> 1–4: using adverbial, non-finite and relative clauses
> 5–6: text structure; paragraphs
> 7–10: uses of a colon

1 The book, <u>which he found on the table</u>, was now useless to him.

2 <u>As the wind whispered gently</u>, Lydia fell fast asleep.

3 They emerged from the cave, <u>blinking in the sunlight</u>.

4 Which subordinate clause begins with: **a conjunction?** _2_   **a relative pronoun?** _1_   **a non-finite verb?** _3_

5 You are writing a non-fiction text. What might be the most likely cue for starting a new paragraph in

a recount of an event: _Change of time._   **a report on your local area:** _Change of topic._

a discussion: _Change of viewpoint._

6 Give three ways in which the main point might be developed in the rest of the paragraph

By giving examples, by commenting, by expanding with more detail.

Why has each colon been used?

7 Occupation: musician. _To show that information will follow._

8 The story begins with these intriguing words: 'Once upon a cloud …' _To introduce a quotation._

9 Debris was scattered down the road: bits of metal, a wheel, milk crates. _To introduce a list._

10 His face was red: he had been running. _To link the two statements – the second expands on and explains the first._

Section 2   Test 2

A   WARM-UP

Write four different types of sentence.

1 **active sentence:** The elephant _slurped the water greedily._

2 **passive sentence:** The elephant _was frightened by the mouse._

3 **complex sentence:** The elephant _drank and drank, emptying the lake completely._

4 **exclamation:** The elephant _has escaped!_

Underline the word that is **not** an abstract noun.

5 jealousy courage <u>honest</u> mischief

6 grief anguish distress <u>desolate</u>

7 peace freedom <u>humane</u> equality

> **PART A Focus**
> **1–4:** varying sentence types
> **5–7:** abstract nouns
> **8–10:** spelling strategies; mnemonics

Complete the mnemonic.

8 The _reign_ of a sove _reign_ .

9 Make _sure_ you mea _sure_ it.

10 Always _plan_ an ex _plan_ ation.

B   WORD WORK

1 Add the missing vowel phonemes.

secr e t a ry all e y all er gy cat e g o ry
terr i t o ry estu a ry b uo y comp a ny

Should the word have a hyphen in the middle?
Put a tick or a cross.

2 reaction ✗   **4** nonfiction ✓

3 flowchart ✗   **5** grandfather ✗

6 Write two words to follow the hyphen.

non- _drip_

non- _smoking_

> **PART B Focus**
> **1:** tricky and unstressed vowels
> **2–6:** the use and misuse of hyphens
> **7–10:** homophones

Write a sentence to show the meaning.

7 **course:** _The yacht had to change course to avoid the ferry._

8 **coarse:** _The fabric was coarse – rough and uncomfortable._

9 **sauce:** _Brown sauce is yummy on egg and chips._

10 **source:** _We tracked down the source of the problem._

C   SENTENCE WORK

Complete the sentences, using a different subordinating conjunction in each one.

1 _Although the boy was a pain,_ Susie felt sorry for him.

2 Susie felt sorry for the boy _because he had no friends._

3 Susie felt sorry for the boy _until she heard what he had done._

Is the semi-colon used correctly? Put a tick or a cross.

> **PART C Focus**
> **1–3:** using subordinating conjunctions
> **4–8:** using semi-colons
> **9–10:** language features; persuasive texts

4 Australia is a great place to live; hot weather and beautiful beaches. ✗

5 The children returned home; they had been away all week. ✓

6 We enjoyed the holiday; despite the weather. ✗

7 I rarely eat fatty foods; occasionally I fancy a cake. ✓

8 Look at the sentences with a cross. In what way has the semi-colon been used incorrectly?
The second part is not a main clause.

You are writing an advertisement. What language features would you use and why?

9 **sentence structures:** _Short sentences for impact; complex sentences to paint a picture._

10 **stylistic techniques:** _Rhetorical questions, commands, emotive language, slogans (using alliteration, repetition, puns, humour) – all for direct communication with the reader._

Section 2   Test 3

A   WARM-UP

Write a question-and-answer joke based on the homonym.

1 **crane:**

Q: What bird works on a building site?

A: A crane.

2 **bank:**

Q: Where does the river keep its money?

A: In the river bank.

Complete the well-known saying.

PART A Focus
1–2: word play; homonyms
3–5: use of apostrophes
6–10: spelling; adding prefixes and suffixes

3 You're a star.

4 Don't blot your copybook!

5 It's not over till it's over.

Complete the word sum.

6 **regret + able + ly =** regrettably

7 **menace + ing + ly =** menacingly

8 **admit + ed + ly =** admittedly

9 **ir + regular + ly =** irregularly

10 **im+ polite + ly =** impolitely

B   WORD WORK

1 Complete the grid.

	+ ed	+ ing	+ al
recite	recited	reciting	recital
bury	buried	burying	burial
refer	referred	referring	referral

2 Add the prefix. **ab ad**

_ad_ join   _ab_ normal

PART B Focus
1: rules for adding suffixes
2–6: the prefixes **ab** and **ad**
7–10: archaic language

Write the meaning of the prefix.

3 **ad:** towards   **4** **ab:** away from

Write four more words that show the meaning.

5 **ab** abduct, abhor, abject, absent

6 **ad** admit, adapt, adhere, adopt

Write a modern question that means the same.

7 Where art thou? Where are you?

8 What would'st thou? What do you want?

9 Who hath dared to wound thee?

Who has tried to hurt you?

10 How are the verbs different in the older version?

They use archaic verb endings such as 'th' and 'st'.

C   SENTENCE WORK

Rewrite the complex sentence, starting with a non-finite verb.

1 As he gathered his strength, he lifted the rock. Gathering his strength, he lifted the rock.

2 Because she was filled with despair, she sat alone. Filled with despair, she sat alone.

3 Although he was groaning with pain, he stood up. Groaning with pain, he stood up.

4 What is the function of these subordinate clauses?

They give information about how the people felt.

Change the sentence to avoid any confusion over the pronouns used.

5 Rik entered Joe's room. ~~He~~ Joe turned to face him.   **6** Ali phoned Lal. He had found ~~his~~ Lal's dog.

7 Hilda and Ethel did not speak. ~~She~~ Hilda took off her coat and made ~~her~~ Ethel do the same.

Add the missing dashes to the sentence.

8 He was tall—twice as tall as Nikki—and wore a long coat.

PART C Focus
1–4: using non-finite clauses
5–7: correcting unclear use of pronouns
8–10: using a pair of dashes for effect

9 Jack was not sure—was not at all sure—what he had seen.

10 Why are the dashes used?

To isolate and emphasise a point in a sentence that is repeated or expanded on.

X DEFINITIVE ANSWER   X SAMPLE ANSWER

Section 2 Test 4

A WARM-UP

Write a sentence starting with the adverb given.

1 Nimbly, *she crossed the bridge.*

2 Viciously, *he stabbed the beast.*

3 Obstinately, *he refused to budge.*

4 Frantically, *they shouted for help.*

Add the same prefix to all three words.

5 *al* ready   *al* mighty   *al* together

6 *a* float   *a* board   *a* broad

7 *re* organise   *re* possess   *re* produce

8 *non-* striker   *non-* smoking   *non-* existent

> **PART A Focus**
> **1–4:** starting sentences with adverbs
> **5–8:** prefixes
> **9–10:** tricky letter patterns

9 Write six words starting with **rh**.

rhyme, rhythm, rhombus,
rhubarb, rhinoceros, rhapsody

10 Add the same missing letter to all six words.

g *u* ard   g *u* ess   g *u* itar

g *u* est   g *u* ide   g *u* ilt

B WORD WORK

Write the words correctly.

1 physicly *physically* basicly *basically*

personly *personally* actuly *actually*

2 laboratry *laboratory* boundry *boundary*

3 machinry *machinery* threatning *threatening*

> **PART B Focus**
> **1–3:** unstressed vowels; syllables
> **4–7:** spelling strategies; antonym prefixes
> **8–10:** using suffixes; changing word class

Write the antonym pair.

4 *Clue:* put together and take to pieces

as / *sem* / *ble*   and   *disassemble*

5 *Clue:* needed and not needed

ne / *ces* / *sa* / *ry*   and   *unnecessary*

6 *Clue:* applicable and not applicable

rel / *e* / vant   and   *irrelevant*

7 *Clue:* lasting and temporary

per / *man* / ent   and   *impermanent*

Add the same vowel suffix to all three words.

8 tour *ist*   special *ist*   extreme *ist*

9 active *ity*   agile *ity*   mobile *ity*

10 What class of words have you made? *nouns*

C SENTENCE WORK

Add a subordinate clause that begins with a relative pronoun.

1 The woman, *whom we called Old Betty,* was working in her allotment.

2 The bus, *which was late,* rattled down the road.

3 Marik and Simon met at Cypress Drive, *where they had last seen Dr Novak.*

4 Stella, *whose clothes were soaked through,* stood in the doorway.

5 Add the punctuation and capital letters.

They froze. *W*hat was that? *W*as it a footstep? *H*ad someone found them? *T*hey hardly dared breathe.

6 What effect has been created – and how? *Fragments make it sound jumpy; questions build anticipation and reflect the uncertainty of the characters.*

> **PART C Focus**
> **1–4:** relative clauses; use of commas
> **5–6:** punctuation; sentence effects
> **7–10:** use of similes

7 Underline the simile.

Angela was sleeping <u>like a kitten</u>, curled up amongst the filthy sacks.

8 Why has the writer chosen this simile? *It makes the character seem innocent.*

Write a simile to make the character sound

9 **pleasant:** Her laugh was *like the peal of bells on a sunny day.*

10 **unpleasant:** Her laugh was *like the cry of a wild animal.*

Section 2   Test 5

A   WARM-UP

Take the noun **car** and modify it to make four different noun phrases.

1 an old car with rusty paintwork

2 the sleek red car in my garage

3 the latest eco-friendly car

4 a vintage car in the museum

5 Underline the unstressed vowel.

parliament   alcohol   diary

chocolate   vegetable

6 Write the words correctly.

natral   _natural_   peple   _people_

dimond   _diamond_   miniture   _miniature_

Add a three- or four-letter word to complete the longer word.

7 po _sit_ ion

8 ex _pans_ ion

9 ent _ran_ ce

10 m _use_ um

> **PART A Focus**
> **1–4:** expanding nouns; noun phrases
> **5–6:** unstressed and unsounded vowels
> **7–10:** spelling strategies

B   WORD WORK

Add **able** or **ible**.

1 ed _ible_   reput _able_

2 leg _ible_   prob _able_

Add **able** or **ible** to the root word.

3 response _ible_   enjoy _able_   identify _iable_

Add the correct 'shun' ending.

4 exclude _sion_   equate _ion_   optic _ian_

> **PART B Focus**
> **1–4:** adding able, ible, ion, sion, cian
> **5–8:** everyday and subject-specific words
> **9–10:** suffixes; word classes

Write different definitions for the words in **bold**.

5 It was a **physical** game.

physical: _rough_

6 **Physical** geography.

physical: _dealing with natural features_

7 There was **friction** between the men.

friction: _disagreement and anger_

8 There is **friction** on this surface.

friction: _a force that slows moving objects_

Add the same suffix to all three words, to make nouns that name types of people.

9 chem _ist_   flor _ist_   cycl _ist_

10 vegetar _ian_   librar _ian_   Christ _ian_

C   SENTENCE WORK

Oscar had to leave. He was tortured by his memories.

Rewrite the two sentences as one. Do so in four different ways.

1 Oscar had to leave as he was tortured by his memories.

2 Tortured by his memories, Oscar had to leave.

3 Oscar, tortured by his memories, had to leave.

4 Because he was tortured by his memories, Oscar had to leave.

Add the punctuation and capital letters.

5 "Take it," she said. "It's worthless now."

6 "My big regret," sighed Mr James, "is losing the medal."

7 "I'll never," she said with dignity, "leave Park Street."

8 "My work is complete," said Merlin. "Now I must leave."

9 Cross out the words that are not Standard English. Write them correctly.

We ~~was~~ winning ~~easy~~. It was a ~~real~~ good game.   _were, easily, really_

He saw ~~them~~ cards ~~what~~ you dropped but he didn't do ~~nothing~~ to help.   _those, that, anything_

10 Give two examples of places where it might be appropriate to use non-Standard English in writing.

In direct speech in a story; in a transcript.

> **PART C Focus**
> **1–4:** forming and punctuating complex sentences
> **5–8:** speech punctuation
> **9–10:** Standard English

X DEFINITIVE ANSWER   X SAMPLE ANSWER

Section 2   Test 6

A   WARM-UP

Write one shorter and one longer version of this sentence.

Close by, a tawny owl hooted.

> PART A Focus
> 1–2: varying sentence length
> 3–5: spelling strategies
> 6–10: adverbs; synonyms; word meanings

1 An owl hooted.

2 Suddenly, from out of the darkness, a tawny owl hooted mournfully.

Add a three- or four-letter word to complete the longer word. The shorter word starts with

3 **d:** con _den_ sation   in _dust_ ry   evi _den_ ce

4 **p:** re _pet_ ition   hap _pen_ ed   pro _port_ ion

5 **m:** di _men_ sion   per _man_ ent   to _mat_ oes

Write two synonyms.

6 **nonchalantly**   casually, coolly

7 **furtively**   secretively, stealthily

8 **haughtily**   arrogantly, conceitedly

9 **jovially**   pleasantly, genially

10 **obstinately**   stubbornly, adamantly

B   WORD WORK

Add **ei** or **ie**.

1 perc _ei_ ve   n _ie_ ce   p _ie_ rce   dec _ei_ ve

2 s _ei_ ze   w _ei_ r   prot _ei_ n   n _ei_ ther

3 The words in 2 are tricky because they don't follow the normal 'i' before 'e' rule.

4 Add the suffix **ous**.
nerve ous   outrage ous   vigour ous

5 Add the suffix **ity**.
mobile ity   able ility   generous ity

6 Add the suffix **al**.
industry ial   face ial   nature al

Write a definition.

> PART B Focus
> 1–3: ei and ie spellings
> 4–6: spelling patterns; adding suffixes
> 7–10: defining words from context

7 The path **petered out**.
petered out: came to an end

8 The **mesmerising** beat began again.
mesmerising: captivating; hypnotic

9 The portrait is **enigmatic**.
enigmatic: mysterious; puzzling

10 The event **culminated in** a disco.
culminated in: came to a climax with

C   SENTENCE WORK

Why has the writer used the passive form?

1 A man was killed in the incident. To avoid saying who was responsible

2 The diamond was stolen. The writer doesn't know, or doesn't want to say, who stole it.

3 The parcel was delivered. It does not matter who delivered it.

4 The King was warmly applauded. The King is the key focus, not the people applauding him.

Add the apostrophes.

> PART C Focus
> 1–4: using the passive voice to suit purpose
> 5–7: using the apostrophe
> 8–10: avoiding ambiguity

5 Brunel's ship is one of Bristol's main attractions.

6 You'll find the children's playground behind Fisherman's Cottage.

7 Both clubs' managers are waiting to hear the FA's decision.

Rewrite the sentence to avoid ambiguity.

8 I saw a motorbike with a young man riding it with gleaming chrome.
I saw a young man riding a motorbike with gleaming chrome.

9 The class visited a bakery to see bread being made on Wednesday.
On Wednesday, the class visited a factory to see bread being made.

10 That's the man with the dog who used to have a moustache.
That's the man who used to have a moustache, with the dog.

Section 2   Test 7

| A | WARM-UP |

Continue the sentence in different ways.

1 Joe wanted to believe her – he truly did.

2 Joe wanted to believe her though he knew something was not quite right.

3 Joe wanted to believe her because she looked so helpless.

4 Joe wanted to believe her but how could he?

Add the missing letters.

PART A Focus
1–4: sentence variation
5–6: tricky letters y and i
7–10: spelling words by syllables; once and ence

i y

5 paral _y_ se   real _i_ se   c y cl _i_ st   d _i_ et

6 c _i_ nders   t _y_ p _i_ cal   d _i_ sk   ph _y_ s _i_ cal

Add the missing syllables.

7 per / _for_ / mance   *Clue: a show*

8 ap / _pear_ / ance   *Clue: how things look*

9 ev / _i_ / dence   *Clue: proof*

10 cir / _cum_ / _fer_ / ence   *Clue: perimeter*

| B | WORD WORK |

Write three words ending with

1 **eight:** weight, freight, sleight

2 **aught:** caught, naught, fraught

PART B Focus
1–2: letter strings
3–6: prefixes
7–10: subject-specific use of words

Make three words by adding prefixes to the root word.

3 **active** reactive, inactive, proactive

4 **face** deface, interface, preface

5 **scribe** describe, subscribe, inscribe

6 **claim** exclaim, proclaim, reclaim

Write sentences to show the different meanings of each word.

7 **freeze** (in science): Water freezes when the temperature reaches freezing point.

8 **freeze** (in drama): When you hear the knock at the door, you should freeze.

9 **fibre** (in food): Foods such as bread and cereals contain plenty of fibre.

10 **fibre** (in D&T): In this fabric the fibres are loosely woven.

| C | SENTENCE WORK |

Add a relative clause.

1 His coat, which had been hanging by the door, was gone.

2 Jenny, who was tired and frustrated, snapped at her brother.

3 In the forest, where darkness came quickly, all was not well.

4 What is the purpose of a relative clause? To give extra information about a person, item or place.

PART C Focus
1–4: using relative clauses
5–8: colon to link clauses
9–10: use of pronouns

Add a colon and a second clause that expands on the first.

5 It was his first victory: the first of many.

6 She spoke calmly: she had regained her composure.

7 Olivia was silent: nobody had spoken to her like that before.

8 The ground was dusty and cracked: there had been no rain for over a month.

Mrs Modi and her neighbour were talking. She was almost deaf so she had to speak up. She was telling her about her cat.

9 Why is this confusing? Overuse of pronouns means it is not clear who is being referred to.

10 Rewrite the text above so that the meaning is clear. Mrs Modi was telling her neighbour about her cat. The lady was almost deaf so Mrs Modi had to speak up.

X DEFINITIVE ANSWER   X SAMPLE ANSWER

Section 2 Test 8

A WARM-UP

Create an acrostic phrase or sentence for the word

1 **snow:** _softness now over the world_

2 **dawn:** _day awaking with newness_

3 **stream:** _Streams tumble, rushing eagerly_
down a mountainside.

4 Add the prefix.

PART A Focus
1–3: manipulating word order
4–7: prefixes
8–10: visual spelling strategies

a ab ad

_a_ drift   _a_ light   _ab_ olish   _ad_ opt

Add the correct antonym prefix.

5 *Clue: in maths*

_a_ symmetrical   _ir_ regular   _un_ equal

6 *Clue: in PE*

_in_ active   _non_ -striker   _im_ mobile

7 *Clue: in science*

_in_ vertebrate   _ir_ reversible   _in_ soluble

Add the same three- or four-letter word to complete all three longer words.

8 con _cent_ rate   in _cent_ ive   inno _cent_

9 am _ate_ ur   m _ate_ rial   cre _ate_

10 awk _war_ d   re _war_ d   s _war_ m

B WORD WORK

Underline the word that is wrongly spelt.

PART B Focus
1–4: pluralisation
5–6: tricky spellings
7–10: word structure; word meanings

1 chiefs <u>shelfs</u> beliefs reefs

2 scarves leaves <u>rooves</u> halves

3 tomatoes heroes volcanoes <u>patioes</u>

4 radios <u>echos</u> cellos ratios

One consonant or two? Add the missing letters.

5 a _cc_ o _mm_ odation   di _s_ a _pp_ oint

6 emba _rr_ a _ss_ ment   reco _mm_ end

Underline the prefix and write the root word.

7 <u>tele</u>communications   _communicate_

8 <u>em</u>bolden   _bold_

Write a definition.

9 **telecommunications:** _ways of_
communicating over long distances

10 **embolden:** _to make bold_

C SENTENCE WORK

Use commas to separate the different parts of the sentence.

1 After the clock struck, that was when he first heard it, the unmistakable sound of fear.

2 At the end of the corridor, half-hidden in the murky light, a hunched figure began to move.

3 There, advancing towards him, at a pace and with growing excitement, was Sir Galahad.

4 How does the way the sentences are written build up tension? _They have three parts that build up_
slowly to the main action. The main focus is hidden or delayed until the end.

The fog wrapped itself darkly around the choking streets.

PART C Focus
1–4: using sentence structure and punctuation for effect
5–8: personification
9–10: formal impersonal style

5 What technique has the writer used? _personification_

6 What is its effect? _It makes the fog seem sinister._

Complete the sentence and create a similar effect.

7 The ice _attached itself to the windows, trapping them inside._

8 The sun _glowered down angrily, with a heat that shrivelled the flowers._

Express these ideas in a formal and impersonal style.

9 I hope you learn from this mistake. _It is to be hoped that lessons are learned from_
this mistake.

10 Let's discuss this big issue. _This major issue deserves careful consideration._

Section 2   Test 9

A   WARM-UP

Add a relative clause containing additional information.

1 Emily, _who is tone deaf,_
wants to be a singer.

2 The ruby, _which was as big as a plum,_
glinted in the sunlight.

3 The street, _which had been busy,_
was now deserted.

Write the word that has **both** meanings.

4 _fret_ : to worry/a part of a guitar

5 _reserve_: to set aside/a substitute

6 _fire_ : to dismiss from employment/a blaze

Continue the compound word chain.

7 touch**down** – **down**fall – _fallback_

8 may**fly** – _flyover_ – _overcoat_

9 over**lap** – _laptop_ –
topside – _sideways_

10 ear**ring** – _ringleader_ –
leadership – _shipmate_

PART A Focus
1–3: relative clauses
4–6: homonyms
7–10: compound words

B   WORD WORK

1 Add the letter(s) that make the 'sh' phoneme.

i _ss_ ue   ma _ch_ ine   ra _t_ io   an _c_ ient

Add a 'shun' suffix and write the new word.

2 **repeat** _repetition_   **3** **reveal** _revelation_

4 This suffix turns the verbs into _nouns._

5 Add the same two letters to all the words.

frant _ic_   tact _ic_   electron _ic_

6 Add one or more extra suffixes to each word.
frantically, tactical, electronically

7 Add a suffix that makes the words into verbs.

critic _ise_   public _ise_   character _ise_

8 Write each word with a different suffix.

critic _al_   public _ation_   character _istic_

Write a definition.

9 **eco-tourist:** _a traveller who is concerned about the environment_

10 **cyber-criminal:** _someone who commits crimes using the internet_

PART B Focus
1: tricky phonemes
2–8: suffixes to modify words
9–10: word meanings; prefixes

C   SENTENCE WORK

PART C Focus
1–4: varying the position of subordinate clauses
5–7: stylistic features
8–10: using semi-colons

Move the subordinate clause to the start of the sentence.

1 The old woman shouted at the driver because she was angry.
Because she was angry, the old woman shouted at the driver.

2 The boy followed her, dragging the bag. _Dragging the bag, the boy followed her._

3 Sophie, who was hidden from view, felt safe. _Hidden from view, Sophie felt safe._

4 In which sentence did you have to change the wording slightly and why?
In 3, because it was a relative clause and wouldn't make sense at the start.

Read this car advert. **Advanced design + innovative technology = optimum aerodynamic performance**

5 Describe the target audience. _Car lovers with lots of money, who want high performance cars._

Explain two stylistic techniques used to appeal to this target audience.

6 _Vocabulary that sounds technical and cutting edge._

7 _Written as an equation rather than as a sentence to give a hi-tech feel._

Use a semi-colon to continue the sentence.

8 There was an ornate box in the corner of the room; _Sophie had not noticed it before._

9 She looked again; _the boy had gone._

10 The boy would not jump; _he was scared of the water._

X DEFINITIVE ANSWER   X SAMPLE ANSWER

Section 2 Test 10

A WARM-UP

Expand the nouns to provide information about the character.

1 farmer: _the white-haired farmer by the gate_

2 lady: _the old lady in the tweed suit with baggy pockets_

3 puppy: _the sad-eyed puppy that followed me to school_

4 detective: _the smartly dressed detective with the shiny shoes_

Add the same suffix to make all three words into adjectives.

5 athlete _ic_   gymnast _ic_   energy _etic_

6 express _ive_   decorate _ive_   figure _ative_

7 danger _ous_   nerve _ous_   hazard _ous_

Add a three- or four-letter word to complete the longer word.

8 de _fin_ ite

9 des _pair_ ing

10 s _old_ ier

> **PART A Focus**
> 1–4: noun modification
> 5–7: adding suffixes to modify word usage
> 8–10: spelling strategies

B WORD WORK

1 Write the correct spelling.

vegetariun _vegetarian_ religun _religion_

knowlidge _Knowledge_ texchure _texture_

2 Write one other word with the same ending as each of the four words above.

guardian, region, pledge, capture

Change the suffix to make another word.

3 identity _ify_

4 comprehension _ive_

5 alliteration _ive_

6 investigation _ive_

> **PART B Focus**
> 1–2: word endings
> 3–7: using suffixes to modify words; word derivations
> 8–10: working out meaning from context

7 Write three words derived from the word **compete**.

competition, competitor, competitive

Write a definition of the word in **bold**.

8 His face was **contorted** with pain.

contorted: _twisted_

9 As the tide went out the water **receded**.

recede: _retreat; go back_

10 It is time to **implement** the plan.

implement: _bring into practice_

C SENTENCE WORK

Make the sentences impersonal by rewriting them in the passive form.

1 We recorded the information on the database. _The information was recorded on the database._

2 We will provide all meals. _All meals will be provided._

3 You must return your application form by Friday. _Application forms must be returned by Friday._

4 We gently heated the solution. _The solution was heated gently._

5 Punctuate the sentence.

"I'm telling you, he was right there," said Jenny, pointing to the empty armchair.

6 What is the purpose of the last part of the sentence? _The action helps bring the scene to life._

Continue the sentence, combining dialogue and action.

> **PART C Focus**
> 1–4: passive voice
> 5–8: speech punctuation; integrating speech and action
> 9–10: using modal verbs for changes in meaning

7 "Take it," _said Oliver, holding out the last dry crust._

8 "Excuse me," _said Edwina politely, tapping the gentleman on the shoulder._

Allowing pupils to wear their own clothes to school <u>could</u> create a competitive environment.

9 Underline the modal verb.

10 Why has the writer used it? _It makes the argument sound like a possibility rather than a fact. It helps distance the writer from the argument._

Section 2 Test 11

A WARM-UP

Open this sentence in three different ways.

1 *Anxiously,* _____

Josh glanced up.

2 *Hearing a sound,* _____

Josh glanced up.

3 *As Oscar entered the room,* _____

Josh glanced up.

Continue the compound word chain.

4 hence**forth** – **forth**with

– *without* – *outside*

5 whenever – *evermore*

– *moreover* – *overall*

6 therefore – *forehand* – *handrail*

– *railway* – *wayward*

7 forehead – *headlamp* – *lamplight*

– *lighthouse* – *housefly*

Underline the hidden four-letter word.

8 I C H F X L E **D I E T** A R

9 A E N **A X I S** M U Z T R S

10 E N T I O S O **R O L E** M

PART A Focus
1–3: varying sentences
4–7: compound words
8–10: visual spelling strategies

B WORD WORK

Add the missing syllables to complete the noun.

1 con / *cen* / *tra* / tion **Clue:** *total focus*

2 pre / *par* / *a* / tion **Clue:** *groundwork*

3 con / *den* / *sa* / tion **Clue:** *from gas to liquid*

4 com / *bi* / *na* / tion **Clue:** *mixture*

5 Is the hyphen used correctly? Put a tick or a cross.

mock-up ✓ re-act ✗

non-smoking ✓ a-lot ✗

6 Write the incorrect words correctly.

react, a lot

PART B Focus
1–4: spelling strategies; syllables
5–6: use and misuse of hyphens
7–10: definitions of new words

Write a definition.

7 **podcast:** *broadcast available on demand over the internet*

8 **blogger:** *a person who runs a weblog ('blog'), which is an online diary*

9 **cybercafé:** *a café where you can surf the internet*

10 **wiki:** *a website that can be updated by visitors*

C SENTENCE WORK

Rewrite the sentence so that the main focus comes at the end.

1 A sad cry came echoing over the hills. *Echoing over the hills came a sad cry.*

2 The ghost was there, beside the door. *There, beside the door, was the ghost.*

3 The Prince was sat calmly reading. *Sat calmly, reading, was the Prince.*

Clouds paused; the river chuckled; the wind played with the reeds.

4 Describe the mood of this sentence. *Pleasant and peaceful.*

5 How is this effect created? *Through the choice of verbs and the use of personification.*

Write similar sentences to create a mood that is

6 **sinister:** *Clouds scowled; the river mumbled; the wind bullied the reeds.*

7 **frantic:** *Cars raced; traffic lights blinked; lorries screeched at each other.*

Correct the punctuation.

8 In the 1960's, Dad's favourite programme was Doctor Who.

9 The club has lost two of it's best players.

10 Do'nt knock on stranger's doors.

PART C Focus
1–3: varying sentence structure for effect
4–7: personification; language choice
8–10: the use and misuse of apostrophes

X DEFINITIVE ANSWER X SAMPLE ANSWER

Section 2 Test 12

A WARM-UP

You are describing a deserted beach. Write under each heading two phrases that you could use.

1 sounds: *softly sighing sea; whisper of the wind*

2 textures: *melting dunes; coarse sand between your toes*

3 sights: *white-crested waves; cliffs that are jagged against the sky*

Write the adverb that means

4 with fury: *furiously*

5 with suspicion: *suspiciously*

6 with anxiety: *anxiously*

7 with mystery: *mysteriously*

8 with malice: *maliciously*

> **PART A Focus**
> 1–3: noun modification; descriptive phrases
> 4–8: spelling using root words and suffixes
> 9–10: word structure; related words

Complete the words by adding different affixes and/or root words.

9 *auto* graph graph *eme* *bio* graph *y*

10 *pro* verb verb *al* *ad* verb *ial*

B WORD WORK

Write the words correctly.

1 cathederal dergree specterum
cathedral, degree, spectrum

2 apperatus carberhydrate develerpment
apparatus, carbohydrate, development

3 Are the words spelt correctly? Put a tick or cross.

discuss ✓   disappoint ✓

disolve ✗   discide ✗

4 Write correctly the words that are wrongly spelt.
dissolve, decide

5 Add the suffix that will make the words into verbs.

mod *ify*   simpl *ify*   qual *ify*

6 Add the suffix that will change the verbs into nouns.

modification, simplification, qualification

Write the full version of the word.

7 **lab** *laboratory*

8 **demo** *demonstration*

9 **exam** *examination*

10 **app** *application*

> **PART B Focus**
> 1–4: correcting common spelling errors
> 5–6: suffixes; changing word class
> 7–10: shortened forms; spelling

C SENTENCE WORK

1 Punctuate this sentence.

"Oh, really," he replied, sneering at the figure trembling before him.

2 What is the purpose of the last part of the sentence?

The description of the man's actions helps to portray his character.

> **PART C Focus**
> 1–4: integrating and punctuating speech in longer sentences
> 5–10: opening adverbs; viewpoint

Continue the sentence, combining dialogue and action.

3 "I've some bad news," *Mrs Bains said softly, placing her hand on mine.*

4 "Stop right there," *he commanded, his eyes flashing with anger.*

Continue the sentence as if you were writing to persuade.

5 Obviously, *the situation cannot continue.*

6 Regrettably, *few seem willing to help.*

7 Admittedly, *it will be expensive at first.*

Continue the sentence as if you were writing a newspaper report.

8 Tragically, *Benji, Mr Nick's dog, did not survive.*

9 Luckily, *Jed had a mobile phone and was able to contact his girlfriend.*

10 What is the purpose of these adverbs?

They show the attitude of the writer to what he or she is writing.

Remind the pupil to complete Section 2 of the Progress chart on page 46 of the workbook.   29

Schofield & Sims English Skills 6

Section 2 Writing task assessment sheet: The nervous cyclist

Name		Class/Set
Teacher's name		Date

Sentence structure and punctuation

	Always/often	Sometimes	Never
Varies sentence length (e.g., short for pace and suspense; complex to slow and describe)			
Varies sentence type for effect (e.g., occasional question or exclamation)			
Controls placement of adverbials; expanded phrases or clauses add detail			
Varies word order to create different effects (e.g., bringing feelings to the fore, repetition)			
Uses punctuation to show boundaries between sentences and clauses			
Punctuates dialogue correctly			
Sometimes integrates speech into longer sentences (e.g., combining it with action)			
Uses sophisticated punctuation (e.g., dash, colon, semi-colon)			
Uses punctuation for particular effects (e.g., to slow, draw attention, make contrasts)			

Composition and effect

Writing displays a definite genre (e.g., in description of characters, setting, a key event)			
Combines action, description and dialogue to create an arresting opening			
Uses narrative devices (e.g., clues about how the story might continue, deliberate withholding of information, narrative 'hook')			
Shapes events into linked paragraphs of varying length/structure			
Uses pronouns clearly and without ambiguity			
Uses stylistic devices and figurative language to engage reader or create mood			
Uses imaginative vocabulary for effect			

Spelling

Regular polysyllabic words spelt correctly			
Words with unstressed vowels spelt correctly			
Complex regular spelling patterns accurate			
Common roots, prefixes and suffixes are spelt correctly (e.g., **tion**, **able**, **ible**)			
Rules for adding suffixes are correctly applied and common exceptions recognised			
Uses hyphens and apostrophes correctly			

From: **English Skills 6 Answers** by Carol Matchett (ISBN 978 07217 1186 7). Copyright © Schofield & Sims Ltd, 2011. Published by Schofield & Sims Ltd, Dogley Mill, Fenay Bridge, Huddersfield HD8 0NQ, UK (www.schofieldandsims.co.uk). **This page may be photocopied for use within your school or institution only.**

Schofield & Sims English Skills 6

Section 2 Completed proofreading task: Why we must go green

Name		Class/Set
Teacher's name		Date

Did you know that avrage globel tempratures have increesed by all-most one degree over the past sentury? it doesnt sound like much, does it? but if this trend continnews, it could change Earths climite compltely, threatning our plannet and its frajile eko-systems.

A warmer Earth could permenantly effect many aspects of our plannet: rainfal patturns, sea levels, the ranje of plants and wildlife – even the food we eat and the warter we drink.

When sceintists talk about climite change, there consern is about globul warming corsed by human activitys, yes, thats right, the sauce of the problem is peopel!

You see, burning fuels with carbbon in them (thats oil, gas and coal) adds to the natureal greenhouse layer in the lower atmossfere, trapping more heat and so causeing the earth to warm up.

Cars, airoplanes, power statons and factoryes – they all contrabute to globeal warming, so actuly we are all responsable.

Section 2 tasks summary

From: **English Skills 6 Answers** by Carol Matchett (ISBN 978 07217 1186 7). Copyright © Schofield & Sims Ltd, 2011. Published by Schofield & Sims Ltd, Dogley Mill, Fenay Bridge, Huddersfield HD8 0NQ, UK (www.schofieldandsims.co.uk). **This page may be photocopied for use within your school or institution only.**

Section 3 Test 1

A WARM-UP

Expand the nouns to add more detail to this list of items on a menu.

1 Roast breast of _____ guinea fowl in a pastry crust

2 Goat's cheese _____ salad with sun-dried tomatoes

3 Slow-cooked _____ lamb marinated in a sweet sauce

4 Spiced fillet of _____ salmon baked with aubergines

5 Make three words using these letters and graphemes only. **t b augh ough**

taught, tough, bough

> **PART A Focus**
> **1–4:** noun modification
> **5–6:** spelling; letter strings
> **7–10:** spelling; root words and affixes

6 Add the same grapheme to all the words.

ch orus   ch oir   ch ord   or ch estra

Complete the word sum.

7 in + **access** + ible = inaccessible

8 inter + **nation** + al = international

9 **edit** + or + ial = editorial

10 **civil** + ise + ation = civilisation

B WORD WORK

Add the missing syllables to complete the

1 **abstract nouns:**

gen / er / os / i / ty **Clue:** *kindness*

mis / for / tune **Clue:** *bad luck*

2 **adverbs:**

def / i / nite / ly **Clue:** *without doubt*

ab / so / lute / ly **Clue:** *completely*

3 **adjectives:**

mem / o / ra / ble **Clue:** *unforgettable*

in / no / cent **Clue:** *not guilty*

Write two words derived from the root.

4 **depend** dependable, independent

5 **value** valuable, evaluate

6 **moral** immoral, morality

7 **serve** service, reserve

> **PART B Focus**
> **1–3:** spelling strategies; syllables
> **4–7:** root words; affixes
> **8–10:** subject-specific meanings

Write sentences to show three different meanings of the word **force**.

8 I had to force him to do it.

9 He joined the police force in 2015.

10 Pushes and pulls are forces.

C SENTENCE WORK

Write four sentences using these words only.

read the letter Miss Levy when she was alone smiling to herself

1 When she was alone, Miss Levy read the letter – smiling to herself.

2 Miss Levy read the letter when she was alone, smiling to herself.

3 Smiling to herself, Miss Levy read the letter when she was alone.

4 When she was alone, Miss Levy, smiling to herself, read the letter.

5 Why is the second of these sentences more effective than the first?

Smoking is harmful because it can kill you.   **Smoking is harmful: it can kill you.**

The colon creates a direct link between the cause and the effect and has more impact.

Add a colon and cross out any unnecessary words.

6 There is only one way forward: ~~and that is~~ to cut emissions.

7 You can make a difference: ~~if you~~ join the great recycle.

> **PART C Focus**
> **1–4:** constructing sentences for effect
> **5 7:** using colons
> **8–10:** using connectives; signposting texts

You are writing a discussion text. Give three connecting phrases that would help you to

8 **illustrate a point:** imagine that, supposing, let's say

9 **add another point:** what is more, moreover, in addition

10 **oppose or balance:** however, yet, conversely

X DEFINITIVE ANSWER   **X SAMPLE ANSWER**

Section 3   Test 2

A   WARM-UP

Add a relative clause giving extra information.

1 Try our new range, _which includes many exciting new products._

2 Our products are tested by specialists _____ _who are all experts in the field._

3 This is a product _that will make you feel ten years younger._

Add the missing letters.

4 r u r a l   v o w e l   m a j o r   d i g i t

5 i n d e x   e x i t   a t l a s   u r b a n

6 Underline the words that are wrongly spelt.

<u>modurn</u> <u>patturn</u> trodden flatten

7 Write the correct spelling.

modern, pattern

PART A Focus
1–3: using relative clauses
4–7: spelling strategies; correcting errors
8–10: compound words

Complete the compound word chain.

8 fire**wood** – **wood**wind – _windproof_

9 shorthand – _handbook_ – _bookcase_

10 underpass – _password_ – _wordplay_

B   WORD WORK

1 Write the words as plurals.

prefix	_prefixes_	**cactus**	_cacti_
axis	_axes_	**gazebo**	_gazebos_
video	_videos_	**gateau**	_gateaux_

Add the same prefix to all three words.

2 _anti_ bacterial   _anti_ -racist   _anti_ body

3 _fore_ hand   _fore_ ground   _fore_ cast

4 _sub_ ordinate   _sub_ standard   _sub_ merge

Write three more words with each prefix.

5 _antidote, antihistamine, antipathy_

6 _forearm, forefather, foreword_

7 _submarine, subheading, subway_

PART B Focus
1: pluralisation
2–7: prefixes
8–10: terms of qualification

Write two synonyms of the word(s) in **bold**.

8 It was **mainly** dry.   _mostly, chiefly_

9 It seemed **a little** odd.   _slightly, somewhat_

10 He is **fully** recovered.   _totally, wholly_

C   SENTENCE WORK

The <u>flickering candlelight</u> picked out a long table with heavily carved chairs, an empty fireplace, <u>dusty drapes at darkened windows</u>, portraits of <u>unwelcoming faces</u> – and in the corner amongst the shadows stood a <u>grotesque statue-like figure</u>.

1 Punctuate the sentence.

2 Underline four noun phrases that create a sense of unease.

3 How does the sentence structure contribute to the dramatic effect? _The list of worrying details builds up tension and a frightening figure is introduced at the end._

Continue the sentence, creating a contrast to follow the semi-colon.

4 Latika was successful; _Winston, unfortunately, was not._

5 Mark was always there on time; _Olly sometimes didn't turn up at all._

6 I enjoyed the film; _Beth definitely did not._

7 Reginald Jenkins was born in poverty; _he died a rich man._

Add the correct word. **less fewer**

PART C Focus
1–3: punctuation; sentence effects
4–7: using semi-colons
8–10: using less and fewer

8 I am trying to eat _less_ sugar and drink _fewer_ sugary drinks.

9 There were _fewer_ visitors this year so we raised _less_ money than expected.

10 Many people find they have _less_ time available and attend _fewer_ classes.

Section 3   Test 3

A   WARM-UP

Modify the sentence to create a clear mood.

1 Clouds drift. _Threatening grey clouds drift slowly across the sun._

2 Children scream. _Excited children scream as they jump into the waves._

3 Lights twinkle. _Bright lights twinkle enticingly in shop windows._

What could the word be? Write three possibilities.

4 p_st_l   _pastel, postal, pistol_

5 m_n_s   _minus, mines, manes_

6 d_c_d_   _decide, decade, decode_

Write three synonyms.

7 **anxiously**
   apprehensively, nervously, uneasily

8 **bravely**
   valiantly, courageously, heroically

9 **warily**
   cautiously, suspiciously, hesitantly

10 **nimbly**
   deftly, dextrously, neatly

B   WORD WORK

1 Add the missing letters.

c s cc ss sc

a _cc_ e _ss_   ne _c_ e _ss_ ary   su _cc_ e _ss_

pro _c_ e _ss_   _s_ in _c_ erely   di _sc_ ern

_s_ in _c_ ere   adole _sc_ en _c_ e   de _c_ i _s_ ion

Add the missing syllable or syllables.

2 ac / _ci_ / dent   *Clue: a mishap*

3 dis / _cip_ / line   *Clue: regulation, control*

4 de / _cep_ / tion   *Clue: dishonesty*

5 fas / _ci_ / nate   *Clue: to intrigue*

6 Write one word that is related to each word above.

accidentally, disciplinary, deceptive, fascination

Write a sentence using the word as a verb.

7 **snake:** _The path snakes along the valley._

8 **panic:** _I panicked when I saw the fire._

9 **pilot:** _She piloted the plane to safety._

10 **slave:** _I slaved over that job for days._

C   SENTENCE WORK

Add to the start of the sentence a clause that gives a reason.

1 _To make the event more child-friendly,_ we are planning to hire a juggler.

2 _By obtaining new equipment,_ we hope to improve the centre.

3 _Because of poor weather,_ the work has not yet been completed.

Add the missing punctuation.

4 Di blinked. "Not now," she whispered, shaking her head. "I need time to think."

5 "You," Joel said, pointing to Nigel. "You will pay for this."

6 "I've bin speakin' to t' master," Edgar began.

7 "You ain't comin' in," said Mrs Noon, barring the door.

Write the opening sentence for a mystery story.

8 **dialogue:** _"I don't think we should be here, Lewis," whispered Lucy._

9 **short sentence:** _The door was already open._

10 **complex sentence:** _Darkness had already cloaked Granger Avenue when the alarm pierced the silence._

Section 3   Test 4

A   WARM-UP

Continue the advertisement choosing suitable words.

1 Experience the West Indies: _beautiful beaches, vibrant culture_

2 Safeguard your skin: _Keep it looking fresh and healthy_

3 Chocolate for grown-ups: _a sophisticated taste for the connoisseur_

Write six words with this ending.

4 **idge** _bridge, porridge, ridge, fridge cartridge, partridge_

5 **age** _average, montage, percentage, voyage, cabbage, luggage_

6 **ture** _nature, capture, manufacture, texture, feature, creature_

Add the missing letters.

7 l y r i c

8 v i r u s

9 m e t h o d

10 m o d e m

> **PART A Focus**
> **1–3:** emotive vocabulary; adjectives; nouns
> **4–6:** common word endings
> **7–10:** spelling strategies

B   WORD WORK

Cross out the words that are wrongly spelt.
Write the correct spelling.

1 The ~~sucsess~~ of the ~~sceme~~ depends on this ~~facter.~~ _success, scheme, factor_

2 This ~~isshue~~ ~~shuold~~ remain ~~seperate.~~ _issue, should, separate_

3 In ~~genral,~~ results of the ~~trile~~ were ~~encurageing.~~ _general, trial, encouraging_

> **PART B Focus**
> **1–3:** recognising and correcting spelling errors
> **4–7:** word roots
> **8–10:** defining words using context

Write a word that begins with the root.

4 **mono** _monopoly_   **5** **corp(us)** _corpse_

Write the meaning of the root.

6 **mono:** _single_   **7** **corp(us):** _body_

Write a definition of the word in **bold**.

8 Their movements were **synchronised**.
synchronised: _deliberately made to occur at the same time_

9 It was just about **tolerable**.
tolerable: _bearable; not bad, but not good_

10 The artist character is a **stereotype**.
stereotype: _a fixed set of ideas about a particular kind of person or thing_

C   SENTENCE WORK

Police catch man with butterfly net
Stolen car abandoned by river

School dinners protest
Medics help snake bite victim

1 Why are the newspaper headlines confusing? _Their brevity makes them ambiguous._

Write each headline as a clear and complete sentence – as if it were in the main part of the article.

2 _The police have caught a man who was carrying a butterfly net._

3 _A stolen car was abandoned near to the river by the thieves._

4 _There has been a protest about school dinners._

5 _Medics helped the victim of a snake bite._

Add brackets within the sentence.

6 I wouldn't help him for a million pounds (although the money would be rather tempting).

7 Katie volunteered (what a surprise) to help.

8 I said the car was definitely blue (that's correct, isn't it?) and old.

9 What do the brackets contribute to the tone of the sentence?
The change in tone is contained within them.

> **PART C Focus**
> **1–5:** recognising and avoiding ambiguity
> **6–9:** using brackets
> **10:** imagery; alliteration

10 Continue the sentence using imagery and alliteration.
Outside _the traffic rumbled and rattled, moving like a giant machine._

X DEFINITIVE ANSWER   X SAMPLE ANSWER

Section 3 Test 5

A   WARM-UP

Write three sentences using the word **carrot**, to appear in

1 **a newspaper:** Mr Das won first prize for his superb display of carrots.

2 **instructions:** Slice the carrot and add it to the onion.

3 **a story:** Mr Rae had a nose shaped like a carrot.

4 Underline the words that are spelt correctly.

<u>design</u> desease <u>deny</u> dessolve devide

5 Write correctly the words that are wrongly spelt.

disease, dissolve, divide

Add a second syllable.

> **PART A Focus**
> **1–3:** varying sentences to match text types
> **4–7:** spelling errors; spelling strategies
> **8–10:** common roots

6 hic / cup

7 tis / sue

Add the same root word to all three words.

8 re quest   quest ionnaire   quest ion

9 un know n   know ledge   know ing

10 port folio   pass port   port er

B   WORD WORK

Add the correct ending.

> **PART B Focus**
> **1–3:** word endings; making choices
> **4–5:** prefixes
> **6–10:** word meanings; different contexts

1 **ance ence**

bal ance   prefer ence   relev ance

2 **ent ant**

relev ant   independ ent   adjac ent

3 **ar er or**

gramm ar   offend er   trait or

Write three words beginning with

4 **uni:** unison, unify, universe

5 **multi:** multiply, multiplex, multiple

Write different definitions of each word.

6 **cell (in IT):** a space on a spreadsheet

7 **cell (in biology):** one of the units that make up living things

8 **cell (in everyday use):** a room in a prison

9 **monitor (in IT):** a computer screen

10 **monitor (verb):** to check regularly

C   SENTENCE WORK

1 Punctuate the sentence with commas and a semi-colon.

Springing to her feet, Angela's expression clouded, anger flickering in her eyes; she grabbed her coat, let out a tirade of abuse and stormed out of the door.

2 What is the effect of this sentence construction? It helps to build a sense of Angela's anger.

3 Compose a similar sentence describing a desperate search.

Angela searched the desk, opening drawers, scattering the papers; she emptied the folders, leaving a heap on the floor.

Briefly explain how the idea is different in each of the sentences.

4 **I must go to the gym later.**   It is a necessity.

5 **I might go to the gym later.**   It is a possibility.

6 **I will go to the gym later.**   It sounds definite.

7 **I should go to the gym later.**   It is a duty, but the writer is not keen to go.

8 **I can go the gym later.**   The writer is able to go if he or she wishes to.

> **PART C Focus**
> **1:** using commas and semi-colons
> **2–3:** using sentence construction and punctuation for effect
> **4–10:** modal verbs creating subtle variations in meaning

9 Underline the words above that make the difference between sentences.

10 Rewrite the sentence as a possibility rather than a statement of fact.

Johal was there.   Johal might have been there.

X DEFINITIVE ANSWER   **X SAMPLE ANSWER**

Section 3   Test 6

A   WARM-UP

Complete the complex sentence.

1 I stood on the edge *of the diving board,*
peering down into the blueness.

2 As the rest of the guests chatted and
laughed, *_____* I stood on the edge
of the gathering like a ghost.

Complete the word sum.
Start the sum with an antonym prefix.

3 *im* + **move** + *able* = *immov(e)able*

4 *ir* + **resist** + *ible* = *irresistible*

5 *non-* + **flame** + *able* = *non-flammable*

Write the adverb that means

6 with energy: *energetically*

7 with imagination: *imaginatively*

8 with compassion: *compassionately*

9 with regret: *regrettably*

10 with menace: *menacingly*

B   WORD WORK

Cross out the words that are wrongly spelt in
the headline. Write the correct spelling.

1 ~~Portrate exibition~~ opens at ~~gallary~~
portrait, exhibition, gallery

2 ~~Applorse~~ for ~~amature theater~~ group
applause, amateur, theatre

3 ~~Govament desision 'riddiculus'~~
government, decision, ridiculous

Write two words that begin with the root

4 **bene** (meaning **well**):
benefit, benevolent

5 **bio(s)** (meaning **life**):
biography, biodegradable

Write sentences to show the different meanings of
these near synonyms for **change**.

6 **alter:** *I'll alter the costume so it fits.*

7 **correct:** *A spellchecker corrects errors.*

8 **vary:** *Vary the shades of blue used.*

9 **reorganise:** *Let's reorganise the team.*

10 **transform:** *Make-up transforms her face.*

C   SENTENCE WORK

1 **The butler lay dead on the floor.**

The butler lay, dead, on the floor.

Why has the writer added the commas? *To isolate the word 'dead' and emphasise the key idea.*

Add commas that perform a similar function.

2 I lay there, terrified, waiting for the noise to stop.

3 They walked, fearfully, into the room.

Write an example of your own.   **4** *He climbed, unwillingly, into the car.*

Why is the headline amusing?

5 Giant police hunt for jewel thief   *It sounds as though large officers are hunting for the thief.*

6 Students make a tasty meal   *It sounds as though someone is eating the students.*

7 Robson's back under pressure   *It sounds as though Robson has pressure on his back.*

Explain two possible purposes of

8 **a leaflet for Town Farm:** *to inform, to persuade*

9 **an eyewitness account of a tornado:** *to recount, to describe*

10 **a newspaper report about a protest march:** *to recount, to comment*

Section 3   Test 7

A   WARM-UP

Continue the sentence.

1 So, I'd failed – *but so had Jessica.*

2 Nobody noticed – *until it was too late.*

Add the missing syllables.

3 un / *for* / *tu* / *nate* / ly
Clue: *unluckily*

4 con / *se* / quent / *ly*
Clue: *as a result*

5 ap / prox / *i* / mate / *ly*
Clue: *about, roughly*

6 Make six words using all or some of these letters and no others. You may use a letter more than once if necessary.

c s u a e i   *success, successes, access,*
issue, case, cause

Add a two- or three-letter word to complete the longer word.

7 em *bar* rass

8 ca *the* dral

9 sy *no* nym

10 be *lie* ve

> **PART A Focus**
> **1–2:** using dashes for effect; sentence construction
> **3–5:** spelling strategies; syllables
> **6–10:** visual spelling strategies

B   WORD WORK

1 Write in the tricky part of each word.

sil _hou_ ette   b _eau_ tiful   man _oeu_ vre

2 Write the correct spelling.

miniture *miniature*   aquired *acquired*

3 Underline the correct spelling.

forfill forfil fulfill fullfil <u>fulfil</u>

> **PART B Focus**
> **1–3:** tricky spellings
> **4–6:** suffixes; word classes
> **7–10:** commonly confused words

Add the suffix that changes the words into

4 **verbs:**   public *ise*   memory *ise*

5 **abstract nouns:** cruel *ty*   scarce *ity*

6 **nouns naming places:** bake *ry*   pot *tery*

Write a sentence to show the meaning of

7 **conscience:** *His conscience was clear.*

8 **conscious:** *He was conscious on reaching hospital, and remembered the crash.*

9 **practise (verb):** *I practise the piano every day.*

10 **practice (noun):** *Nat loves football practice.*

C   SENTENCE WORK

The man fled: he was leaving his home, leaving his possessions, leaving his past behind.

1 Punctuate the sentence using a colon and commas.

Give two techniques that the writer has used to make the sentence effective.

2 *Repetition of the word 'leaving' to emphasise the personal cost.*

3 *Using a list structure that builds up to a climax at the end of the sentence.*

Underline the two verbs that you find the most emotive.

4 kill <u>slaughter</u> execute <u>exterminate</u>

5 cut <u>slash</u> reduce <u>axe</u>

6 chase <u>hound</u> follow <u>stalk</u>

7 Explain why these verbs are emotive.
They carry implications that make the reader respond emotionally.

> **PART C Focus**
> **1–3:** sentence effects; stylistic techniques
> **4–7:** emotive language
> **8–10:** persuasive techniques

Some people want to paint the room red.

Counter this idea with a sentence that

8 **is dismissive:** *These people are clearly deluded.*

9 **uses evidence to refute it:** *However, research shows that over 80 per cent would prefer a neutral colour.*

10 **shows it is a weak idea:** *But red is widely known to be the colour associated with anger.*

X DEFINITIVE ANSWER   X SAMPLE ANSWER

A   WARM-UP

Write a dramatic sentence containing no more than five words.

1 Stella screamed, turned and ran.

2 Then, everything stopped.

3 My time had come.

4 Something had happened – something awful.

Write the word beside its definition.

bilingual cinquain triad unilateral

5 triad — chord of three notes

6 bilingual — able to speak two languages

7 unilateral — one sided

8 cinquain — poem of five lines

> **PART A Focus**
> 1–4: short sentences for impact
> 5–8: word meanings; etymology
> 9–10: words and suffixes; word class

Form ten words using these word parts. Add each word to the correct category.

tour organ vandal bapt ist ism ise

9 **nouns:** baptist, baptism, organist, organism, tourist, tourism, vandalism

10 **verbs:** baptise, organise, vandalise

B   WORD WORK

Write the correct spelling.

1 circumfrance — circumference
isoscelles — isosceles

2 gess — guess
approxamate — approximate

3 avrage — average
devision — division

> **PART B Focus**
> 1–3: correcting spelling errors
> 4–6: root words; derivations
> 7–10: subject-specific meaning of words

Write three words derived from the root.

4 **believe** — belief, believer, disbelief

5 **force** — enforce, reinforce, enforceable

6 **examine** — examination, examiner, examined

Write different definitions of each word.

7 **consumer** (in D&T): someone who buys and/or uses things

8 **consumer** (in science): animal that consumes other living things

9 **producer** (in drama): the person responsible for a production

10 **producer** (in science): a green plant that makes its own food

C   SENTENCE WORK

Rewrite the sentence using a colon for effect.

1 The only hope they had left was the raft. They had only one hope left: the raft.

2 Climate change is a new threat to the survival of animals. Animals are facing a new threat to survival: climate change.

3 Our victory was the result of determination and teamwork. Our victory was the result of two things: determination and teamwork.

> **PART C Focus**
> 1–3: using colons for effect
> 4–7: text signposts
> 8–10: Standard English (spoken and written)

What do the following tell you about what is to come?

4 However, despite some successes … An outline of failures will follow.

5 The main difference between … An outline of the difference between two things will follow.

6 Since then … A description of what has happened more recently will follow.

7 All of these ideas … A summary or a more general point will follow.

Rework the transcript into formal Standard English.

8 We was goin' up town but the fog wus bad. We were going into town but the fog was bad.

9 Her knew a'right, but her din say nothing. She knew of course, but she did not say anything.

10 Me and Jim we both 'ad one of them games what was on the telly. Jim and I both had one of those games that were shown on television.

Section 3 Test 9

A WARM-UP

Complete the sentence.

1 Pausing _for a moment, he checked his_ _watch._

2 Frowning _with concentration, he re-read_ _the letter._

3 Fighting _the urge to run, she peered_ _down the corridor._

Add the correct word.

> **PART A Focus**
> **1–3:** sentences starting with non-finite verbs
> **4–7:** using less and fewer
> **8–10:** using suffixes; changing word classes

less fewer

4 Today, _fewer_ people walk to work.

5 Mrs Jones now has _less_ money.

6 I worked _fewer_ hours; I earned _less_ pay.

7 _Fewer_ cows means _less_ milk.

Make the words into

8 **adjectives:**

space _ious_   allergy _ic_   race _ial_

9 **nouns:**

accurate _cy_   generous _ity_   aware _ness_

10 **nouns:**

assist _ant_   rehearse _al_   attach _ment_

B WORD WORK

Write three words related to the word in **bold**.

1 **prefer**

preference, preferable, preferential

2 **define**

definite, redefine, definable

3 **sign**

signature, design, signal

4 **person**

personal, personality, impersonal

> **PART B Focus**
> **1–4:** word families
> **5–7:** common roots and endings
> **8–10:** defining words; etymology

Write two words ending in

5 **logue:** _dialogue, catalogue_

6 **logy:** _psychology, genealogy_

7 **graphy:** _geography, calligraphy_

Underline the root and write a definition.

8 **deforestation:** _the process of clearing_ _forests_

9 **unsystematic:** _haphazard or random_

10 **aromatic:** _perfumed; fragrant_

C SENTENCE WORK

Hi, Em. You off swimming? Yeah ... no worries. See you tomorrow. About 10.

> **PART C Focus**
> **1–6:** spoken and written language structures
> **7–10:** integrating speech into longer sentences; speech punctuation

What clues tell you that this is spoken language?

1 **word clues:** _Uses informal language and fillers._

2 **sentence clues:** _No complete sentences, interruptions (...)._

3 **content clues:** _Sense isn't entirely clear without context._

I saw Emma earlier. She was carrying her kit bag, which meant she was going swimming. She said she was in a rush so I said I'd meet her tomorrow at 10 a.m.

What clues tell you that this is written text?

4 **word clues:** _Uses full version of Emma's name; no social language; no fillers._

5 **sentence clues:** _Clearly defined full sentences; ideas are linked ('which', 'so')._

6 **content clues:** _Context clear; events made explicit and in past tense; uses reported speech._

Continue the sentence, combining speech and actions.

7 Turning to _face Mac, Adam said, "So it was you all along."_

8 "She's _asking to speak to you," said Ailsa, leading the way upstairs._

9 Aaron _looked round the door and said, "Can I come in?"_

10 "Sir_," shouted Liam, jumping out of his seat. "I know the answer!"_

X DEFINITIVE ANSWER   X SAMPLE ANSWER

Section 3 Test 10

A WARM-UP

Add a subordinate clause.

1 Ricky agreed at once *because he was bored with all the discussion.*

2 Ricky, *who knew time was running out,* agreed at once.

3 *Although he hated Simon,* Ricky agreed at once.

> **PART A Focus**
> **1–3:** varying position of subordinate clauses
> **4–6:** roots, prefixes and suffixes
> **7–10:** spelling strategy; syllables

Make two words by adding different prefixes and suffixes.

4 *ex* press *ion*   *im* press *ive*

5 *de* port *able*   *ex* port *ing*

6 Make the words into verbs.

advert *ise*   solid *ify*   origin *ate*

Add the missing syllables.

7 ma / *te* / *ri* / *al*   *Clue: fabric*
8 dis / *ad* / *van* / tage   *Clue: a drawback*
9 con / *so* / nant   *Clue: not a vowel*
10 ho / *ri* / *zon* / tal   *Clue: not vertical*

B WORD WORK

1 Write the root word.

vegetation   *vegetable*
liquefy   *liquid*
specification   *specify*

Write a definition.

2 **vegetation:** *any form of plant life*

3 **liquefy:** *make into liquid form*

4 **specification:** *an exact description of what is required*

One consonant or two? Add the missing letters.

5 o *cc* a *s* iona *ll* y (c s l)
6 di *s* a *pp* ea *r* ance (s p r)
7 pa *r* a *ll* e *l* (r l l)
8 a *pp* a *r* a *t* us (p r t)

> **PART B Focus**
> **1–4:** identifying roots; working out meaning
> **5–8:** single and double consonants
> **9–10:** terms of qualification

Write three synonyms of the word in **bold**.

9 It was **very** cold.
incredibly, extremely, exceptionally

10 You could hear it **sometimes**.
occasionally, irregularly, now and then

C SENTENCE WORK

That night, they came. That night, they crept closer. That night, they slipped unseen through countless windows.

What techniques has the writer used to build tension?

> **PART C Focus**
> **1–4:** sentence effects
> **5–7:** effect of adverbs
> **8–10:** constructing sentences with a colon

1 Repetition.   **2** Short sentences.

Write a similar set of sentences.

3 Slowly, *the sea advanced. Slowly, the sea inched closer. Slowly, the sea swallowed the sand and the rocks.*

4 Now *he ran. Now he fled. Now he ran through the forest, not daring to look back.*

Underline the adverbs and explain their effect on the meaning.

5 Many children <u>now</u> skip breakfast.   *Suggests that the situation is deteriorating.*
6 <u>Yet</u> we have <u>still</u> had no reply.   *Suggests 'in spite of everything'.*
7 Mrs Bassi was <u>again</u> disturbed.   *Suggests that it is a continuous happening.*

Add a colon and continue the sentence.

8 Everything was in place: *books on shelves, papers filed, folders stacked.*
9 Ajit remembered how it had felt to fly: *weightless, soaring, riding the thermals.*
10 The situation was grim: *there was no way out, she was alone, she had no phone.*

Section 3   Test 11

A   WARM-UP

Write three sentences using the word **mysterious**.

1 newspaper report: _Police are investigating a mysterious burglary._

2 advert: _Explore the mysterious world of Ancient Egypt._

3 description: _The box was engraved with mysterious symbols._

Complete the word sum.

4 graph + _ic_ + _al_ + _ly_ = _graphically_

5 strategy + _ic_ + _al_ + _ly_ = _strategically_

6 _un_ + fortune + _ate_ + _ly_ = _unfortunately_

7 _un_ + emote + _tion_ + _al_ = _unemotional_

Write the word beside its definition.

resplendent multifarious verbose

> **PART A Focus**
> 1–3: sentences matched to text type
> 4–7: adding affixes
> 8–10: using roots to work out meaning

8 _multifarious_ with great variety

9 _verbose_ wordy; long-winded

10 _resplendent_ dazzling, gloriously bright

B   WORD WORK

Add the missing vowels.

1 cap _a_ ble   ed _i_ ble   sol _u_ ble

2 audi _e_ nce   coher _e_ nce   bal _a_ nce

3 haz _a_ rd   meth _o_ d   gramm _a_ r   jarg _o_ n

Write a verb, an adjective and a noun based on the root – and label each one.

4 econ _economise (verb), economical (adjective), economy (noun)_

5 class _classify (verb), classified (adjective), classification (noun)_

6 medic _medicate (verb), medical (adjective), medicine (noun)_

Write different definitions.

> **PART B Focus**
> 1–3: tricky endings; unstressed vowels
> 4–6: suffixes; word classes
> 7–10: subject-specific word meanings

7 solution (in science): _a liquid in which a solid is dissolved_

8 solution (in PSHE): _a way of solving a problem or dispute_

9 tension (in drama and PHSE): _a feeling of nervousness_

10 tension (in D&T and science): _tautness_

C   SENTENCE WORK

1 Punctuate this sentence so that it reads effectively.

She dreamt about a room: an empty room, an empty room with no windows, a room with no way in – and no way out.

> **PART C Focus**
> 1–4: sentence effects; punctuation
> 5–8: Standard and non-Standard English
> 9–10: using pronouns clearly

2 What makes the sentence structure effective?
Information is given in snippets, like a list, to build tension and fear.

3 How does the punctuation help? _The commas slow the pace; the dash makes a dramatic pause._

4 What other technique has the writer used? _Repetition._

Continue the dialogue using Standard English.

5 "Well," _announced Mr Terry. "If you could all follow me I'd be grateful."_

6 Rose _looked up and said, "We would prefer to wait, thank you."_

Continue the dialogue using non-Standard English.

7 "Well," _said Terri. "The coach were delayed so we was all real late."_

8 Rose _continued, "I seen her yesterday, talking with them boys."_

Add a proper noun and a possessive pronoun to complete the text.

9 Len and Joe found the instructions. _Len_ began to read, following the text with _his_ finger.

10 Meanwhile, _Joe's_ eyes flitted from piece to piece, assembling the model in _his_ mind.

X DEFINITIVE ANSWER   X SAMPLE ANSWER

Section 3 Test 12

A WARM-UP

Write an acronym sentence based on the word in **bold**. Then circle the letters that form the acronym.

1 time: *It ⓣicks by ⓘn ⓜoments, ⓔndlessly.*

2 smile: *Ⓢighs Ⓜight turn ⓘnto Ⓛaughs Ⓔventually.*

3 towns: *Ⓣowering Ⓞffice blocks Ⓦatch Ⓝeighbouring Ⓢuburbs.*

Complete the word table.

	verb	adjective	noun
4	exhaust	exhaustive	exhaustion
5	collect	collectable	collection
6	agree	agreeable	agreement
7	impress	impressive	impression

What does the instrument record?

8 thermograph *temperatures*

9 seismograph *earthquakes*

10 chronograph *time*

> **PART A Focus**
> **1–3:** word play; manipulating words
> **4–7:** word classes; suffixes
> **8–10:** working out meaning, using roots

B WORD WORK

Add the correct word.

effect affect

1 Weather conditions may *affect* the results.

2 The change will have an *effect* on us all.

3 I can't let this *affect* my performance.

4 Measles can *affect* the nervous system.

Add the missing vowels.

5 *Clue: nourishing*

n u tr i t iou s

6 *Clue: polite; relating to society*

c i v i l

7 Write two nouns related to each adjective above.

nutrient, nutrition, civilian, civilisation

> **PART B Focus**
> **1–4:** common confusions: affect and effect
> **5–7:** related words; vowels
> **8–10:** defining technical words

Write a scientific definition.

8 germ: *a micro-organism that causes disease*

9 vertebrate: *an animal with a spine*

10 microclimate: *the climate of a small area*

C SENTENCE WORK

They called the man Jack. ~~yes~~ᴛ, that was right. ~~but~~ᴮ what was the other man's name? ~~he~~ᴴ was sure it was a name he knew; it was floating tantalisingly in his mind, just out of reach. ~~wait~~ᵂ a moment—come on—yes, William: that was it.

1 Add punctuation and capital letters to make the passage read effectively.

2 What effect is created by the sentence structure? *The sentences reflect the character's thoughts.*

3 Continue the text with another sentence. *But what use were their names now?*

Strengthen the argument by adding a phrase or clause after the noun.

4 Parents *who are concerned about their children's health* demand answers.

5 All people *who love animals* should protest.

6 Anyone *with a love of nature* will be appalled at this decision.

7 Local residents *, incensed by the situation,* are writing to the council.

> **PART C Focus**
> **1–3:** sentence effects
> **4–7:** post modification of nouns
> **8–10:** poetic forms and language

Write the first two lines of a

8 ballad: *The night was dark and it was still; Then a clatter of hooves came over the hill*

9 haiku: *Waves wash smooth the sand, Leaving no trace of footprints.*

10 limerick: *There was a young man from Torquay, Who had never been in the sea.*

Schofield & Sims English Skills 6

Section 3 Writing task assessment sheet: Launchpad local

Name			Class/Set	
Teacher's name			Date	

Sentence structure and punctuation

	Always/often	Sometimes	Never
Varies sentence length and type			
Extends sentences using conjunctions, adverbials and relative clauses			
Constructs sentences to express subtleties (e.g., uses passives and conditionals)			
Manipulates word order for emphasis and effect			
Uses a variety of verb forms, including imperatives, different tenses and modals			
Uses punctuation to mark boundaries between sentences and clauses			
Uses sophisticated punctuation (colon, semi-colon, brackets)			
Uses punctuation to create particular effects (e.g., colon to omit words or link ideas)			

Composition and effect

Selection and organisation of content informed by purpose and needs of reader			
Organises ideas into coherent sequence of paragraphs, arranged for effect			
Each section has a clear focus and is introduced and concluded appropriately			
Tone is persuasive, engaging and appropriate to the reader (e.g., uses informal comments)			
Uses appropriate stylistic devices (e.g., rhetorical questions, emotive language)			
Gives key points more emphasis through use of expanded noun phrases and adverbials			
Develops clear viewpoint that anticipates reader's reactions, pre-empting comments			

Spelling

Polysyllabic words spelt correctly			
Words with unstressed vowels spelt correctly			
Knows complex spelling patterns			
Chooses and spells correctly common roots, prefixes and suffixes (e.g., **tion**, **able**, **ible**)			
Applies rules for adding suffixes and knows exceptions			
Uses hyphens and apostrophes correctly			
Corrects single/double consonant confusions			
Irregular words spelt correctly			

Schofield & Sims English Skills 6

Section 3 Completed proofreading task: Megan's mystery

Name		Class/Set	
Teacher's name		Date	

The cori͏door was diserted, the classrooms ~~was~~ diserted, their ~~was~~ no movments, no voises, no sounds of eny sort: it was as if the school had been mommenterilly frozern in time.

Megan had just one thorght: to find the diary. she had spent all day perswading herself that this was defernatly the only way. Obviusly, if Mr Neil caght her, she would have to take the conceequences. that was the risk – a risk she was prapared to take. it was her only chanse, was'nt it? it was a neccesery risk.

Cautiusly, she stole down the corridor, nerveusly checking the libruary before reaching Mr Neils room. she entered. buisnesslike, she headed straght for Mr Neils desk, searching with concenttration, folowing her carefulyplaned stratigy, leaveing no evidense.

Then, suddenlly – what was that.? Footsteps, voises … a voise she recergnised – right outside the door! she froze, terryfied, waiting to be disscoverd.

Section 3 tasks summary

Full list of the Schofield & Sims English Skills books

Workbooks

For Key Stage 2:

English Skills 1	978 07217 1175 1
English Skills 2	978 07217 1176 8
English Skills 3	978 07217 1177 5
English Skills 4	978 07217 1178 2
English Skills 5	978 07217 1179 9
English Skills 6	978 07217 1180 5

The same workbooks, with covers designed for older users – at Key Stage 3 and beyond:

Essential English Skills 1	978 07217 1188 1
Essential English Skills 2	978 07217 1189 8
Essential English Skills 3	978 07217 1190 4
Essential English Skills 4	978 07217 1191 1
Essential English Skills 5	978 07217 1192 8
Essential English Skills 6	978 07217 1193 5

Answers

Suitable for use with both **English Skills** and **Essential English Skills**:

English Skills 1 Answers	978 07217 1181 2
English Skills 2 Answers	978 07217 1182 9
English Skills 3 Answers	978 07217 1183 6
English Skills 4 Answers	978 07217 1184 3
English Skills 5 Answers	978 07217 1185 0
English Skills 6 Answers	978 07217 1186 7

Teacher's Guide

The **Teacher's Guide** contains the **Workbook descriptors**, **Entry test** and many other useful items suitable for use with both **English Skills** and **Essential English Skills**:

| English Skills Teacher's Guide | 978 07217 1187 4 |

Also available

Mental Arithmetic (for Key Stage 2) and **Essential Mental Arithmetic** (for Key Stage 3 and beyond) are similar in format to **English Skills** and **Essential English Skills**, providing intensive maths practice.

For further information about both series, and for details of the **I can do** teaching method, which can be used with all the books mentioned on this page, visit **www.schofieldandsims.co.uk**